ENDORSEMENTS

Setting Captives Free is one of the most comprehensive books I've ever read concerning the ministry of deliverance. Jake Kail has brought our vital call to "cast out demons" into the light—free from the apprehensions and misunderstandings that have kept us from confronting darkness head-on. Our church, along with many other churches in our region, has benefitted greatly from Jake's ministry. "Deliverance" is no longer a shrouded, back-room brawl with evasive spirits. Instead, setting people free from spiritual bondage has become a powerful component in our ministry life. I highly recommend this book!

DR. DAVE HESS
Pastor of Christ Community Church
Camp Hill, Pennsylvania
Author of *Hope Beyond Reason*; *Hope Beyond Disappointment*; and
Side by Side: Women and Men Leading Together in the Church

Jake Kail's *Setting Captives Free: How to Break the Chains of Demonic Influence* is one of most thoroughly written manuscripts on deliverance that I have ever read. He profoundly surveys the Old and New Testament Scriptures, capturing the true essence of the ministry of deliverance and revealing that it is a central emphasis of Jesus' ministry for us today. In this book, Jake does an excellent job dispelling many of the modern-day myths and misconceptions on the subject matter, arming you with revelatory insights and a solid biblical foundation in helping you to understand, against popular beliefs, that deliverance is in fact another aspect of healing.

In *Setting Captives Free*, you will discover and learn that casting out demons was a normal occurrence in Jesus' ministry and a byproduct and proof of the Kingdom of Heaven being present. Jake Kail, who is an emerging apostolic leader, shares that deliverance was not just another side issue, but a vital aspect of what Jesus Christ taught, demonstrated, and imparted to His followers. The Church, and every believer then and now, is to continue in setting captives free according to Luke 4:18-19.

I highly endorse and recommend this powerful deliverance manual from my friend who has masterfully and carefully written with you in mind. It is both an invaluable tool and a spiritual weapon for leaders, believers, and successive generations to recognize demonic entrances, influences, and manifestations in order to minister in the supernatural ministry of setting captives free!

DR. NAIM COLLINS
President, Naim Collins Ministries
Wilmington, Delaware
Author of *Realms of the Prophetic*

Jake Kail has done a masterful job in simplifying this sometimes-controversial topic. *Setting Captives Free* is a book that anyone young or old can read and understand God's heart for each believer to walk in wholeness and freedom. Jake's compassion for people to walk in freedom is felt throughout each chapter. This book will empower and equip you to walk in freedom and learn how to set others free. It is one of the best books on deliverance I have read!

ELIZABETH TIAM-FOOK
Founder, International Young Prophets
Santa Rosa Beach, Florida

Jake Kail has been a minister of deliverance for years. His experience, wisdom, and concern are quite evident within the pages of this book. He is passionate about seeing both believers and nonbelievers set free from the clutches of the devil. This is quite evident when perusing his latest literary work. In *Setting Captives Free*, Jake takes us on a journey into a world where deliverance is not always commonplace, but should be. He emphasizes the significance of this vital ministry for today's generation. Jake sounds the alarm, alerting those under demonic oppression that there is a path to total liberation. Jake brings illumination to that path through concise tenets and persuasive examples. His approach is biblical and practical, giving the reader a solid foundation to assist them on their way to total liberation through Jesus Christ. He lavishly utilizes Scripture as an underpinning throughout the chapters.

Within this book, Kail assists the reader in demystifying deliverance ministry, provides keys for receiving deliverance, explains how demons get in, and much, much more! There are also breakthrough prayers and anointed declarations that are mandated to free you and your loved ones. This is a book that causes satan to tremble at the very thought of it getting into your hands! It is written in a compacted yet exhaustive style, loaded with content but extremely reader-friendly.

I love how Jake includes actual testimonies of people who received tremendous freedom from demonic influence and opposition. He is a very transparent, intelligent, and effective writer. As you read *Setting Captives Free*, you can literally feel the author's heart regarding those who are in bondage to the hordes of hell. He is very serious about getting them set free. There is a genuine concern here for the natural and spiritual health of the reader that feels tangible. I can hear chains breaking in the spirit and falling off due to the anointing that rests upon this great work. Don't miss the great opportunity to add this book to your arsenal as another weapon to be used to bankrupt hell by setting the captives free!

Dr. John Veal
Author of *Supernaturally Delivered* and *Supernaturally Prophetic*
Johnveal.org

I love my friend Jake Kail's new book, *Setting Captives Free*. This book contains a desperately needed message for today's Church: how to find freedom from the influence of evil spirits. Jake draws from his own life and from the Word of God, showing us how every person can find freedom, and then teaches us to do the works of Jesus—casting out demons. God is restoring the biblical truth of casting out demons through His Church today. *Setting Captives Free* is a gift to our generation as our God restores the ministry of deliverance to the Church!

LARRY KREIDER
DOVE International Director and author

Jake Kail is a gift to the Body of Christ and provides a clarion call to awaken the Church to the freedom available through deliverance. He brings clarity and practical understanding to a topic that has been disregarded by so many. *Setting Captives Free* is a helpful tool for your own healing and provides answers to effectively minister deliverance to others. I highly recommend this book! It is power-packed with truth, experience, and testimonies to secure our freedom.

I thank God for Jake and his heart to transform the Body of Christ in the area of deliverance. He has ministered effectively and powerfully at Gateway House of Prayer the past few years, setting many captives free!

BONITA KEENER
Director, Gateway House of Prayer

Setting Captives Free is not merely an exhaustive commentary filled with information. It was written with the intention of being used as a handy, user-friendly, easy-to-read reference guide full of divine impartation to assist believers in destroying the works of darkness. Jake Kail is an apostolic voice and leader who has released a timely arsenal to equip, educate, and empower the body of Christ in living victorious as warriors of the cross. *Setting Captives Free* shares practical and effective strategies, spiritual truths, and biblical realities taken distinctively from the ministry of Jesus, His apostles, and the first-century New Testament church era. This power-packed literary work simply positions every Spirit-filled believer on the offense rather than defense. Jake's book gives the reader a clear spiritual advantage over the enemy.

Setting Captives Free helps you cast off the darkness and walk in the Light because deliverance is the "children's bread" for *all* God's people (see Matt. 15:22-28). In addition, it exposes and dismantles present-day myths on the subject of deliverance with present-day biblical truth to commission believers to walk in the supernatural power of God while breaking demonic influences, torment, oppression, strongholds, curses, and so much more in their lives. I highly recommend and endorse the pages of this book for every believer, church, smallgroup study, and leadership team ready to break every chain holding one's destiny, purpose, and God-given gifts captive.

Dr. Hakeem Collins
Prophetic voice, author, international speaker
Author of Heaven Declares, Prophetic Breakthrough, Command Your Healing, and 101 Prophetic Ways God Speaks

Many are searching for freedom and God is ready to set us free. While people try all kinds of things to find freedom, the biblical answer of deliverance is powerful and effective. But it is often overlooked because of our anti-supernatural bias. Satan uses a variety of means to oppress people and Jake Kail covers them all in *Setting Captives Free*. This comprehensive manual on deliverance is great for those looking for personal freedom or for those who want to gain the understanding needed to help others. Even the appendix section is a valuable reference guide with prayers and other practical helps. This book is a great resource for the body of Christ!

Dr. Barry Wissler
President of HarvestNet International

Setting Captives Free is authentically penned through life experiences and systematic biblical knowledge and wisdom. Jake Kail lays the groundwork for our legal positioning and skillfully reveals how freedom can become our experiential reality. Courage to believe and partner with Heaven's progressive purpose is awakened in us, for us, and ultimately through us for others. I personally know the harassment of shame and fear but also how deliverance released a double-portion inheritance in my life. My journey to health could have been accelerated if *Setting Captives Free* was in my hands all those years ago. Jake is truly a champion of God's justice, equipping us individually and corporately to walk in freedom.

Dr. Melodye Hilton
Author of *Higher Living Leadership* and *Unmasking Prejudice*

Jake Kail is a trusted minister and man of God who was truly born for such a time as this. His passion to see the body of Christ walk in wholeness and holiness bleeds through every page of this book. With a gift for writing and many powerful stories, you will be deeply stirred to walk in a greater realm of freedom than ever before. I wholeheartedly endorse not only this message, but the man who wrote it, for he has become the message and it's evident to all who come into contact with him. Get ready for CHANGE!

Jeremiah Johnson
Bestselling author and speaker
www.jeremiahjohnson.tv

SETTING
CAPTIVES
FREE

SETTING
CAPTIVES
FREE

HOW TO BREAK THE CHAINS OF DEMONIC INFLUENCE

JAKE KAIL

DESTINY IMAGE® PUBLISHERS, INC.
P.O. Box 310, Shippensburg, PA 17257-0310
"Promoting Inspired Lives."

This book and all other Destiny Image and Destiny Image Fiction books are available at Christian bookstores and distributors worldwide.

Cover design by Eileen Rockwell
Interior by Terry Clifton

For more information on foreign distributors, call 717-532-3040.
Reach us on the Internet: www.destinyimage.com.

ISBN 13 TP: 978-0-7684-5436-9
ISBN 13 eBook: 978-0-7684-5437-6
ISBN 13 HC: 978-0-7684-5439-0
ISBN 13 LP: 978-0-7684-5438-3

For Worldwide Distribution, Printed in the USA
1 2 3 4 5 6 7 8 / 24 23 22 21 20

DEDICATION

I dedicate this book to those who have been taken captive by the enemy and are in need of deliverance. May the chains of demonic influence be broken from your life even as you read this book. May you be completely set free in Jesus' name!

ACKNOWLEDGMENTS

Thank you to my wife, Anna, for your constant encouragement, love, and support. We have walked side by side in this journey of setting captives free. You are an amazing partner in life, family, and ministry. I love you!

Thank you to Threshold Church for embracing the ministry of deliverance as a normal part of church life and for helping to pioneer this ministry in our region. It is a blessing to serve this church family! And thanks also to Gateway House of Prayer for hosting monthly deliverance services to see more people set free and equipped to minister to others.

Thank you to the Destiny Image team for working with me on this project. Thanks to Larry Sparks, Tina Pugh, and Shaun Tabatt for welcoming me into the DI family. Thank you to all who worked on the editing, design, marketing, and other facets of producing and distributing a book. It's been a joy to work with this great team!

Thank you to the group of intercessors who committed to pray for me and this book throughout the writing and publishing process. Your prayers are appreciated very much!

Above all, thanks to our amazing God who sent His Son to die for us that we might be forgiven, restored, and delivered from the devil's grip. He is still in the business of healing broken hearts and setting captives free!

CONTENTS

Introduction. 1

1. Jesus Came to Set Captives Free. 5

2. Five Truths About Demonic Influence. 19

3. Power and Authority Over Demons 37

4. How to Receive Deliverance 53

5. Forgiveness Opens the Prison Door 69

6. Breaking the Chains of Bondage 79

7. Deliverance from Demonic Oppression 99

8. Set Free from Demonic Torment 111

9. Freedom from the Spirit of Infirmity 121

10. Uprooting Generational Curses and Strongholds . . 131

11. Breaking Word Curses and Severing Soul Ties . . 143

12. Setting Our Children Free 157

13. Established in Freedom. 167

14. Raising Up an Army to Set Captives Free 177

APPENDIX 1 Open Doors to Demonic Influence. 185

APPENDIX 2 What Is the Occult? 189

APPENDIX 3 A Prayer for Deliverance. 195

APPENDIX 4 Biblical Declarations for Walking in Freedom . . . 201

INTRODUCTION

A s the title states, this is a book about *setting captives free*. We will explore what the Bible teaches about demonic influence and how evil spirits gain access into people's lives. And we will learn how to receive deliverance and break the chains of bondage, oppression, torment, and affliction. My goal is not simply to give you information, but to lead you into an encounter with God so that you can step into greater freedom and help others into the same.

The New Testament has many examples of freedom from demonic influence. But many modern believers have struggled to see how the topic of demons and deliverance is relevant to their lives. The Church has often ignored or neglected this topic, or relegated it only to the most extreme of situations. Jesus, however, made deliverance from evil spirits a central part of His earthly ministry. He preached the Gospel of the Kingdom of God, and then He demonstrated the Gospel by healing the sick and delivering the oppressed. He called people to repent and believe the Good News, and He also showed that the Kingdom had come near as a present reality. Casting out demons was a normal occurrence in His ministry and a by-product of the Kingdom of Heaven being at hand. It was not a side issue, but a vital aspect of what He came to do. He also passed this ministry on to His followers and commissioned the Church to continue to set captives free. But in much of the Western Church, the ministry of deliverance has been lost or forgotten. Thankfully, this is changing. There is a fresh awakening happening in the Church regarding the reality of evil spirits and the need to cast them out.

Demons can impact a wide range of areas in our lives. Our spiritual growth, physical health, emotional and mental well-being, and relational dynamics can all be affected by demonic influence. Because of this, the ministry of deliverance can have a far-reaching impact. We must clear away the confusion, misunderstanding, and fear of this topic so that many more captives can be set free.

Obadiah 1:17 says, "But on Mount Zion there shall be deliverance, and there shall be holiness; the house of Jacob shall possess their possessions." This passage gives a progression of how God establishes His people, just like when He first established Israel. He delivered them from the bondage of Egypt, then He set up the law and called them to holiness, and then He led them into the Promised Land to "possess their possessions." Before Israel could walk in holiness to the Lord or enter into their inheritance, they had to be set free from slavery. Deliverance was a necessary step in the process of their destiny, but it was not the end goal. In the same way, believers will not be able to grow in the Lord and walk in the fullness of His plan for them if areas of their lives are still in captivity to the enemy. If the Church is to be all that it is called to be, we must break free from the shackles that bind us. A Church in chains will not be able to advance the Kingdom of God on the earth or be able to fully emerge as the body of Christ to the world.

Jesus is still setting captives free and breaking the chains of demonic influence. Many are seeking help, but don't know what to do or where to turn. I pray that this book will be a resource to facilitate the process of deliverance for you and many others. Throughout the book I have included prayers for deliverance that will help break chains and bring freedom. You can use these prayers for yourself or when praying for others in need. I have also included many modern-day testimonies of freedom from demonic captivity because I want to demonstrate that deliverance from evil spirits is very real and very relevant for today. If you are in need of deliverance, turn your heart to the Lord, let the Holy Spirit lead you, and call on the name of Jesus. He will break the chains and set you free!

. . .

Please note that in the stories throughout this book, all names have been changed in order to protect privacy.

| 1 |

JESUS CAME TO SET CAPTIVES FREE

One of my greatest passions is to see captives set free. There is nothing like seeing chains of demonic oppression, torment, bondage, and affliction loosed from people's lives. In many cases, those set free had been bound in spiritual shackles for many years. They had assumed that they would always have to live with these chains, and resigned themselves to a life of turmoil and defeat. But God had other plans. He stepped in with His grace and mercy, broke through the fetters, and set the prisoners free. This should not surprise us in the least; it is a part of the glorious Gospel of Jesus Christ.

When we read the Gospel accounts, it doesn't take long to see that central to the mission of Jesus was to *set captives free*. Shortly after He began His earthly ministry, He spoke these words, first recorded in the book of Isaiah:

The Spirit of the Lord is upon Me,

Because He has anointed Me

To preach the gospel to the poor;

He has sent Me to heal the brokenhearted,

To proclaim liberty to the captives

And recovery of sight to the blind,

To set at liberty those who are oppressed;

To proclaim the acceptable year of the Lord (Luke 4:18-19).

If Jesus had a mission statement for His earthly ministry, this would be it. We will come back to this passage several times throughout this book. Sometimes we'll look at it in Luke and sometimes in Isaiah, in order to draw out some of its specific nuances.

Jesus called people to repent from sin, believe the Good News, and step into the Kingdom of God. And not only did Jesus preach the Gospel, He demonstrated the Gospel by healing the sick and setting captives free. He confronted powers of darkness wherever He went, breaking the chains that had kept people bound. Freedom is a central part of the Gospel. And one of the reasons I am so passionate to see others set free is because of my own testimony of deliverance from captivity.

My Freedom from Captivity

My parents became believers when I was very young, and I grew up in a wonderful Christian home. I attended our local church regularly, heard the Gospel, and considered myself a Christian. I never questioned the facts of who Jesus is, how He died on the cross for our salvation, and how belief in Him is the only way to Heaven. But I did not have a living relationship with God and I had a shallow understanding of salvation. And beginning in my middle school years and into high school, I was deceived by sin. I was exposed to pornography by a classmate in sixth grade and a seed of sexual immorality was planted. I was drawn into drinking and partying in high school, but still lived under my parents' roof, so I felt restricted.

When I went to college, I no longer had my parents watching over me and giving me consequences for poor choices. I thought this was freedom. I was a freshman at Johns Hopkins University and part of the football team. I went headlong into the party lifestyle, all the while attending Bible studies with a campus ministry and church services on Sunday mornings. I didn't think twice about going to a Bible study and then getting drunk with friends and going out to a club to party. I didn't feel guilty about drinking and engaging in sexual sin on a Saturday night and playing on the worship team at church on Sunday morning. I was living a double life without even knowing it. I was terribly deceived.

Not only is sin deceptive, it is enslaving. It seeks to bind and control us, and the more we give ourselves to it, the more imprisoned we become. I was becoming more and more a prisoner of sin and deception as my freshman year in college continued. At the end of that school year, I was invited to go on a retreat with the campus ministry that I had been attending. Little did I know that my life was about to be drastically changed by a powerful encounter with God.

The retreat was several days long. We did an intensive study through the first half of the Gospel of Mark during the day and worship sessions every evening. People were worshiping the Lord freely during these worship times, singing out and lifting their hands to God. But I couldn't seem to engage. I was stifled and bound, and the atmosphere of freedom around me made this all the more obvious. During the Bible study times, the Holy Spirit began to convict me of my sinful lifestyle. My eyes began to be opened to the double life I was living, and there was a battle raging in my mind. I was coming to a fork in the road, being drawn by God on one hand and tempted by the devil on the other. I knew I couldn't continue to live the way I was living and had to make a choice. On the last night of the retreat, I finally came to a point of surrender.

I asked the leader of our group if I could talk to him in private and began to pour out my heart. I was weeping as I confessed my sin to him and prayed for forgiveness and cleansing. I experienced godly sorrow over sin and a deep work of repentance, and I felt the love of God coming into my heart as I turned to Him. It was so real, so personal, and so powerful. And in the process of this encounter, chains and shackles of bondage were powerfully broken off of my life. A pull toward sexual fantasy, pornography, or any type of sexual sin was completely gone. I had no desire to drink alcohol, get drunk, or engage in the party scene. Sin had lost its hold on me and my desire was to know God and share Him with others. I was set free and my life has never been the same!

Called to Deliverance Through a Dream

Before I knew anything about the ministry of deliverance, I had a passion to see Christians walking in the freedom that Jesus purchased for us on the cross. Because I had been so powerfully set free from the grip of sin, I had a desire to see other believers experience this same kind of liberty. However, I had no idea that casting out demons had anything to do with helping believers gain freedom. My church upbringing did not include the supernatural gifts of the Holy Spirit or the reality of healing and deliverance for today. And my freedom had come without any mention of evil spirits or prayers for deliverance (though looking back, I have no doubt that I was sovereignly delivered from unclean spirits in that encounter). I had always assumed that a true Christian could not have a demon. When I read the accounts of Jesus casting out evil spirits, I believed that they were true, but I was not sure how they were applicable to me or fellow believers.

My journey into the ministry of deliverance started with a simple question: How come everywhere Jesus went He cast demons out of people, and yet I have not seen this happen even one time in going to church my whole life? I asked this question in a conversation with a good friend during my junior year in college. I wasn't so much expecting to find the answer from my friend, who was a fairly new believer with little church experience. The question was more of a reflection on some things I had been pondering. I had similar questions about healing as well. The bottom line was that I knew something was not adding up when I compared the ministry of Jesus with my current Christian life and church experience.

That night I had a vivid dream in which I cast a demon out of someone. The setting of the dream was an all-you-can-eat buffet restaurant. I arose from my table to get more food from the buffet, and on the way I noticed a man with a very dark appearance and an evil look in his eyes. When I sat back down, the man started to walk directly toward my table. I stood up, and as I did I felt the power of God well up within me, giving me a supernatural boldness. I instantly perceived that the man had an evil spirit, and with this fresh empowerment from the Lord, I commanded the demon to come out of him in Jesus' name. The demon left the man through his mouth with a heave. Once the demon was gone, the man's countenance changed, he was filled with joy, and he thanked me for casting it out.

I awoke from this dream with a clear sense that it was from the Lord, but I did not know what to do with it. I actually became concerned that I might soon run into the demonized man I had seen in the dream! The prospect of confronting a demon was not appealing to me, nor did I feel the least bit equipped to do so. Sure, I knew in my mind that the name of Jesus was all-powerful. But *me?* Casting out a demon? Certainly not! Even still, I believed that this dream was part of God's answer to the questions I had been asking.

I began to have other dreams of a similar nature, where I would find myself casting demons out of people. Because deliverance was not part of my church upbringing, I didn't have any biblical foundations in this area and had never seen it modeled. But God has a way of equipping us through various means. During this time, I happened to be browsing through books at a Christian bookstore when a particular title stood out to me. It was called *They Shall Expel Demons* by Derek Prince. I immediately remembered the original dream I had and decided to purchase it. This book was very eye-opening for me. The clear scriptural teaching coupled with the amazing stories of deliverance was a convincing combination. I had a newfound understanding, saw things in a new light, and felt more equipped to cast out demons. Not long after this, I began to pray for people who needed deliverance and see them set free from demonic influence.

I have now been actively ministering deliverance for many years. I minister in personal prayer ministry settings as well as retreats, conferences, and churches. I teach and equip others to minister deliverance and have a passion to see this ministry restored to the Church. It is certainly not the only focus of my ministry, but has been a consistent and fruitful part. Because of my church background, I saw myself as an unlikely candidate to be used in deliverance, but God had other plans. You too can experience God's freedom and be equipped to set others free.

Jesus, the Deliverer

As was the case with me, for many believers in the Western Church deliverance from evil spirits is a foreign concept. We read about it in the New Testament accounts, but don't see it happening in many churches, and so we don't understand how it is relevant to our lives. But for Jesus, deliverance was completely normal. In fact, when He began His earthly ministry, it was His authority to cast out demons that first caught people's attention. The passage below is an account that demonstrates this:

> *Then they went into Capernaum, and immediately on the Sabbath He entered the synagogue and taught. And they were astonished at His teaching, for He taught them as one having authority, and not as the scribes. Now there was a man in their synagogue with an unclean spirit. And he cried out, saying, "Let us alone! What have we to do with You, Jesus of Nazareth? Did You come to destroy us? I know who You are—the Holy One of God!" But Jesus rebuked him, saying, "Be quiet, and come out of him!" And when the unclean spirit had convulsed him and cried out with a loud voice, he came out of him. Then they were all amazed, so that they questioned among themselves, saying, "What is this? What new doctrine is this? For with authority He commands even the unclean spirits, and they obey Him." And immediately His fame spread throughout all the region around Galilee* (Mark 1:21-28).

Jesus was preaching and teaching in the synagogue when the people recognized something different about Him: His teaching carried *authority*. His words had a weightiness they were not used to hearing from the scribes and teachers of the law. The power and anointing with which Jesus taught began to stir up the demonic; a man with an unclean spirit suddenly burst into a manifestation and cried out, "Let us alone!" The demons knew who Jesus was before anyone else did. They wanted to be left alone, but Jesus would not comply. He commanded the evil spirit to be quiet and come out of the man. With a violent convulsion and a loud cry, the demon left the man and he was set free.

The people were astonished. They were aware of the reality of evil spirits, and their religious leaders even had methods and rituals by which they attempted to free people from their influence. But never before had they seen this type of authority. Jesus gave a direct command to the demon, and to their shock, the demon obeyed. Soon, everyone was talking about the new Rabbi who had power over evil spirits. That very evening crowds gathered to His door, seeking to be healed of diseases and set free from demons. They were not disappointed: "Then He healed many who were sick with various diseases, and cast out many demons..." (Mark 1:34).

A few verses later, Mark 1:39 goes on to summarize the ministry of Jesus like this: "And He was preaching in their synagogues throughout all Galilee, and casting out demons." This verse puts the ministry of casting out demons side by side with preaching. Deliverance from demons was not a rare activity only reserved for the most extreme of situations. It was everyday life and ministry, a normal part of the Gospel of the Kingdom that Jesus preached. Deliverance was an open demonstration of the defeat of satan, showing that Someone greater was here. It was part of the reason that Jesus came—to destroy the works of the devil (see 1 John 3:8).

The Freedom We Are Promised

We are promised great freedom in the Gospel of Jesus. The nature of our salvation is multifaceted, and the blood of Jesus is more powerful than we know. Consider Colossians 1:13-14: "He has delivered us from the power of darkness and conveyed us into the kingdom of the Son of His love, in whom we have redemption through His blood, the forgiveness of sins." Redemption, forgiveness, and deliverance from the kingdom of darkness. Look also at how Jesus described how the Gentiles would receive salvation through Paul's apostolic ministry: "to open their eyes, in order to turn them from darkness to light, and from the power of Satan to God, that they may receive forgiveness of sins and an inheritance among those who are sanctified by faith in

Me" (Acts 26:18). Notice that while these verses above include forgiveness of sin, they don't stop there. As amazing as forgiveness is, our salvation contains so much more.

Through the finished work of Christ on the cross, believers are promised freedom from:

1. **The penalty of sin:** "For the wages of sin is death, but the gift of God is eternal life in Christ Jesus our Lord" (Romans 6:23). We are to live with the weight of sin lifted off of our shoulders, knowing that we are totally forgiven because of the blood of Jesus.

2. **The power of sin:** "For sin shall not have dominion over you, for you are not under law but under grace" (Romans 6:14). We are not to be enslaved by sin, and we are not to be bound by addictions. We are to be able to walk in holiness by the grace of God working within us.

3. **The curse of the law:** "Christ has redeemed us from the curse of the law, having become a curse for us (for it is written, 'Cursed is everyone who hangs on a tree')" (Galatians 3:13). Because Jesus became a curse for us, we are empowered to be free from every generational curse. We are also not to be bound by legalism and other religious bondage such as condemnation and paralyzing guilt.

4. **The dominion of satan:** "He has delivered us from the power of darkness and conveyed us into the kingdom of the Son of His love" (Colossians 1:13). We are to be totally free from the devil's power. We are not to be oppressed by demonic spirits or tormented by the enemy's lies.

The above is not an exhaustive list, but it gives an idea of the freedom we are meant to have in Christ. And this does not even begin to mention what we are saved *into*. In Christ, we are a new creation, saved into a relationship with God, a divine purpose, and so much more.

While we are promised great freedom in Christ, the reality is that many believers are not seeing this in their actual experience. In other words, what they have *legally* they do not have *experientially*. So, we often reduce the Gospel message to only include forgiveness and assume that we will live the rest of our lives in some type of bondage or oppression. We believe the lie that we can't really expect to be free on this side of eternity. Instead of seeing freedom as the norm, we lower the bar and expect people to live in captivity, even using religious language to enable it: *That's just your cross to bear. It must be your thorn in the flesh. You can't expect to really be free; we're all sinners after all.*

Do you really believe that Jesus died on the cross so that we could obtain relief from guilt but continue to be enslaved by sin and bound by oppression and torment? This is certainly not God's plan. While we will not be perfect and we will certainly experience trials and difficulties, we are clearly called to walk in liberty. No matter what chains may be keeping you in captivity, this is not how you have to remain. Do not settle for anything less than freedom!

Factors for Freedom

If freedom is the biblical norm and Jesus paid the price for it on the cross, why are so many Christians not experiencing the reality of this freedom? One of the simple reasons for this dissonance is that many believers are under demonic influence and in need of deliverance. Throughout this book, we will consider how casting out demons is a powerful way to set captives free and break chains that enslave. Without the ministry of deliverance, many people will not experience the full freedom that God intends for them to walk in. However, I certainly don't want to give the impression that deliverance from evil spirits is the only aspect of getting free from bondage, oppression, torment, or affliction. On the contrary, there are various factors that can be involved, and everyone's journey is unique. We should be careful not to have a formulaic approach or assume everyone's experience of salvation and freedom will look just like our own.

Like my own testimony, many people have experienced break-through and liberty from sin through encounters with God and deep works of repentance. Some emphasize the need for renewing our minds, being rooted in our identity in Christ, and believing and standing in the truth. Others highlight inner healing and restoring the broken places in our soul. Some have found that after a power-ful baptism of the Holy Spirit, they were delivered from oppression and bondage that formerly enslaved them. Some are set free through a process of time as they immerse themselves in the Word of God and embrace the reality of the cross. Some have a deep revelation of the grace of God and experience the tangible love of the Father and find that chains that used to bind them are no longer there, and they are free from torment and fear.

Everything in the above paragraph is valid, and we should be careful not to diminish one emphasis in order to validate another. An emphasis on deliverance does not invalidate the need to be rooted in love and established in our identity. Repentance and renewing the mind does not negate the need for inner healing or deliverance. Perhaps you were set free through the breaking of a generational curse, but that doesn't mean that this will be the key for everybody else's freedom. We must embrace all of these valid forms of minis-try, and in fact they are all meant to work together. Let's be grounded in the Word and led by the Holy Spirit, and let's leave room for God to work in a variety of ways. While the main emphasis of this book is deliverance from evil spirits, be aware that everyone's journey is unique and there are various ways that God brings freedom, healing, and restoration to people.

He Sets Captives Free!

We serve the God who loves to open prison doors and set captives free. Jesus came to destroy the works of the devil and to redeem us with His own precious blood. He came to deliver us from the penalty and power of sin, and pull us out of the kingdom of darkness. He came to make us new creations, established as sons and daughters of the living God. There is no need for us to stay in captivity any longer.

Sometimes we end up in a spiritual prison because we have been deceived by the lies of the evil one and pulled into bondage to sin. Sometimes we are taken captive through terrible trauma and abuse we have endured. Sometimes we are bound and oppressed because of our rebellion and dismissal of God's Word and God's ways. But no matter how we end up in captivity, Jesus paid the price for our liberty. When we humble ourselves, come to Him in repentance, and call on His name in faith, there is healing and freedom.

As we come to the close of this chapter, take time to slowly meditate on the words of Psalm 107. It will prepare your heart to step out of captivity and into freedom.

Oh, give thanks to the Lord, for He is good!
For His mercy endures forever.
Let the redeemed of the Lord say so,
Whom He has redeemed from the hand of the enemy,
And gathered out of the lands,
From the east and from the west,
From the north and from the south.
They wandered in the wilderness in a desolate way;
They found no city to dwell in.
Hungry and thirsty,
Their soul fainted in them.
Then they cried out to the Lord in their trouble,
And He delivered them out of their distresses.
And He led them forth by the right way,

That they might go to a city for a dwelling place.

Oh, that men would give thanks to the Lord for His goodness,

And for His wonderful works to the children of men!

For He satisfies the longing soul,

And fills the hungry soul with goodness.

Those who sat in darkness and in the shadow of death,

Bound in affliction and irons—

Because they rebelled against the words of God,

And despised the counsel of the Most High,

Therefore He brought down their heart with labor;

They fell down, and there was none to help.

Then they cried out to the Lord in their trouble,

And He saved them out of their distresses.

He brought them out of darkness and the shadow of death,

And broke their chains in pieces.

Oh, that men would give thanks to the Lord for His goodness,

And for His wonderful works to the children of men!

For He has broken the gates of bronze,

And cut the bars of iron in two.

Fools, because of their transgression,

And because of their iniquities, were afflicted.

Their soul abhorred all manner of food,

And they drew near to the gates of death.

Then they cried out to the Lord in their trouble,

And He saved them out of their distresses.

He sent His word and healed them,

And delivered them from their destructions.

Oh, that men would give thanks to the Lord for His goodness,

And for His wonderful works to the children of men!
Let them sacrifice the sacrifices of thanksgiving,
And declare His works with rejoicing (Psalm 107:1-22).

| 2 |

FIVE TRUTHS ABOUT DEMONIC INFLUENCE

Jesus came to set captives free and He has made the way for us to walk in liberty. As believers in Christ, we are not to be bound by sin or shackled in chains of oppression or torment. There may be times of struggle and battle, but freedom should be the norm. There are various factors in our journey into freedom, and throughout this book we will primarily explore how the topic of deliverance from evil spirits relates to this.

The subject of deliverance garners a wide variety of responses. Some would rather not even think about it, deeming it to be too dark, daunting, or depressing. Some are fearful of the topic and avoid it altogether, while others are overly fascinated by it. Many people are entirely skeptical of any such talk, considering the concept of evil spirits to be superstitious, outdated, or simply irrelevant to their lives.

As the Church, it is time to take an honest look at what the Bible teaches us about demons and deliverance from their influence. While we don't need to become fanatical or extreme, we must give this topic the attention that it deserves according to the pattern of Jesus and the early church.

You don't have to dig very deep into the New Testament to discover that casting out demons was a normal practice for both Jesus and His followers. In stark contrast, you often have to search far and wide to find Christians, churches, or ministries that believe in and actively practice the ministry of deliverance today. Even many churches or ministries that affirm the reality of evil spirits and how they can influence people often do not openly teach about or minister in this area.

Because the local church where I pastor openly teaches and practices deliverance ministry, it is not uncommon for us to get inquiries from people living in various places, seeking help in getting free from evil spirits. We have had people from different states and even different countries reach out for help. One woman who lives in a neighboring city told us that out of about 50 churches that she contacted, ours was the only one that responded. This should not be the case! How can something that was so basic for Jesus and the early church be so rare today? Who will help the multitudes of people who are in need of freedom from demonic influence? When will the Church rise up to fill this void and set captives free?

Restoring Deliverance to the Church

Setting captives free and casting out demons go hand in hand. If the body of Christ is going to walk in the fullness of freedom that God intends, we must see the ministry of deliverance fully restored and thriving. As I have already stated, deliverance from evil spirits is certainly not the only factor for walking in freedom. But it is an important component and has often been ignored or neglected by the

Church. In many ways, deliverance has been the missing link when it comes to healing, freedom, restoration, and sanctification.

If we are going to walk in the calling of Jesus to set captives free, we must remove the misunderstanding, fear, and stigma around the topic of deliverance and embrace it in our churches and ministries. If we are going to break the chains of oppression, torment, bondage, and affliction, we will need to include deliverance as a vital part of our arsenal. Deliverance from evil spirits should not be seen as an optional side issue for the Church. It was central to the mission and ministry of Jesus. And when He chose and equipped His disciples, He made deliverance part of their basic training; it was a core class, not an elective.

> *Then He appointed twelve, that they might be with Him and that He might send them out to preach, and to have power to heal sicknesses and to cast out demons* (Mark 3:14-15).
>
> *And He called the twelve to Himself, and began to send them out two by two, and gave them power over unclean spirits* (Mark 6:7).

When Jesus commissioned the Church with the Gospel after He was raised from the dead, He made it clear that deliverance would continue to be a central aspect of the mission: "And these signs will follow those who believe: In My name they will cast out demons" (Mark 16:17). The first sign that Jesus said would follow believers is casting out demons, and yet it is the last thing you will see taught or practiced in many churches. Something is not adding up!

My intention here is not to be critical or judgmental of the Church, but simply to point out the giant gap between what the New Testament describes and our current condition. I believe that if more Christians had a solid understanding of what deliverance is, saw it modeled in a healthy way, and had practical equipping in how to minister it, we could see the ministry of deliverance thriving in the Church and multitudes of people set free.

When Jesus was teaching in a synagogue at the beginning of His ministry, an unclean spirit cried out to Him, "Let us alone!" (see Mark 1:24). Still today, the demons want to be left alone. And whether intentionally or unintentionally, much of the Church has done just that. But we cannot afford to leave them alone any longer. They have been comfortable in our lives, families, and churches for far too long. Like Jesus, we must expose their presence and cast them out. We need to see the ministry of deliverance fully restored to the Church!

Five Truths About Demonic Influence

In order to see deliverance restored, we must eliminate the ignorance and confusion that commonly surrounds this topic. The Bible says that God's people are destroyed for lack of knowledge (see Hosea 4:6). This is certainly true when it comes to the reality of demonic influence and the need for deliverance. Many believers have simply never received any solid teaching in this area. Time and time again I hear people say that they have never heard the topic of evil spirits or deliverance taught in their church. At the same time, people have been exposed to extreme and disturbing Hollywood portrayals. And on top of that, some ministers practice bizarre and unbiblical methods in the name of deliverance. This all leads to much confusion and misunderstanding in the area of deliverance from demons.

There is a great need for clear, scriptural teaching and practice of the ministry of deliverance. This will help remove the barriers and mindsets that keep many people in the dark and unnecessarily bound in chains. The following are five basic truths about demonic influence that will help bring clarity to the topic of deliverance and lay a foundation for stepping into greater freedom.

1. Demonic Influence Is Real

The Bible talks openly about the reality of the spiritual realm. From cover to cover, we see examples of supernatural encounters and spiritual beings. Various types of angels are shown interacting with people to bring messages, protection, and strengthening. Heavenly beings surround the throne of God. We also see fallen angels and demonic spirits bringing temptation, torment, and oppression. And there are many records of supernatural encounters with God, dreams and visions, miracles, signs, and wonders. Although there is some mystery surrounding the spiritual realm, two things are clear: one, it exists; and two, it influences and interacts with the natural realm.

As best as I can tell, the terms evil spirit, demon, and unclean spirit are all used interchangeably in the New Testament. They refer to disembodied spirits of some sort that are in league with the devil and are under his command. These dark spirits are at work in our world and they seek to influence people according to their nature and purposes. I have found that many people in the Church don't want to acknowledge evil spirits as a present and pertinent reality. Many believers will give assent to the existence of demons because they are found in Scripture, but that is where it ends. You can mention the devil and no one thinks anything of it, but when you start to talk about evil spirits, people think you have gone too far!

We cannot afford to turn our heads the other way and pretend that demons are not real or that we never have to think about them. While our primary focus should be on Jesus, we cannot ignore the reality of demonic influence in our world. Demons are real and they seek to influence people in various ways. We were born into a battle, and whether we like it or not, we have a vital role to play in this war. Rather than denying the reality of demonic influence, we should search the Scriptures to determine how evil spirits operate and how to break free from their grip.

2. *Demonic Influence Is Common*

While it is one thing to acknowledge that demonic influence is real, it is another thing to realize that it is actually quite common. Many believers who would never deny the existence of the spirit world and the fact that demons can inhabit or influence people think that it is extremely rare to come across a person needing deliverance. Often this ministry is relegated to the mission field in faraway third world countries. The problem with this thinking is that it does not line up with the ministry of Jesus and example of the New Testament.

We have already seen that deliverance was a central aspect of the ministry of Jesus. Consider this summary of His ministry in Mark 1:39 (NASB): "And He went into their synagogues throughout all Galilee, preaching and casting out the demons." Notice that preaching and casting out demons are put side by side. This pattern can be seen consistently throughout the Gospels. Think about it: *it was as common for Jesus to cast out a demon as it was for Him to preach a sermon!* Far from a rare occurrence, it was everyday life and ministry.

According to the pattern found in the Gospels, we should not see demonic influence or the need for deliverance as a rare or strange occurrence. Because of the confusion, misunderstanding, and lack of experience in the area of deliverance, it can be easy to assume that casting out demons is very rarely needed, especially here in the West. We seldom see it happening and therefore believe that it must not be necessary. This, however, does not line up with what we see in the New Testament, where demonic influence was a very common problem. The fact is, demonic influence was a prevalent issue in the days of Jesus and the early church, and it is a prevalent issue today as well.

Over the last several years of ministering deliverance, I have found that indeed it is very common for people to need deliverance from evil spirits. When I minister in group settings at churches or conferences, I will lead whole groups of people in prayer to receive deliverance.

Many are set free from demonic influence in these settings. My experience and consistent pattern lines up with what is outlined in the Gospel accounts. I propose to you that the reason we do not often see deliverance happening more frequently like in the Gospels is not because the need is not present; it is because we have failed to discern the presence and activity of demons. Many of the issues that people struggle with have an undiagnosed cause—demonic influence. But if we do not consider demonic influence as a potential root, we will not consider deliverance as a potential solution. Therefore, many believers remain in chains.

So, not only is demonic influence real, it is quite common. Many people are in need of deliverance from evil spirits whether they are fully aware of it or not. And as we'll see in the next section, there are varying degrees of demonic influence that a person may be under.

3. There Are Varying Degrees of Demonic Influence

It is important to understand that there are varying degrees of demonic influence. Not every case of demonization and deliverance is the same. Some situations are simple and mild, others are extreme and more complex in nature; and there is everything in between.

There are several factors involved in the degree of demonic influence. One of those factors is the number of demons present. We already saw in Mark 1 how a man in the synagogue was delivered from one unclean spirit. We can see that Mary Magdalene was delivered from seven demons (see Luke 8:2). And the man with the legion of demons most likely had thousands of demons present in him (see Mark 5:1-20). Obviously, the greater number of evil spirits that are present in a person, the more severe the case and the greater degree of demonic influence. Cases like the man with the legion are very rare. But situations like the man in the synagogue or like Mary Magdalene are quite common.

Another factor is the type of demons that are present. The Bible speaks of different kinds of demons, with varying degrees of strength and wickedness. When the disciples failed to cast a demon out of a boy who was tormented, Jesus told them that "This kind can come out by nothing but prayer and fasting" (Mark 9:29). Apparently, this spirit was stronger than others the disciples had cast out previously. Jesus also spoke about some demons being more wicked than others (see Matthew 12:45). The greater the degree of strength and wickedness, the greater the demonic influence will be.

I have also found that in some cases, demons may be present but not have a very strong hold in a person's life. If a person is walking in repentance and living in the light, demons may still be present and need to be cast out, but the level of demonic influence will be less. It is almost as if a demon can sometimes be present but relatively dormant. In contrast, the more a person walks in agreement with sin and the demonic, the more powerful the demonic influence will be. Some demons seem to be deeply entrenched in a person and therefore more difficult to drive out, and there are various reasons why this could be the case.

If I were to tell you that my friend is sick, this could mean a wide variety of things. He could have a 24-hour stomach bug; he could have diabetes; he could be fighting off a fever; he could be dying of heart disease or lung cancer. Just as there is a wide range of physical health problems, there is a wide range of demonic influence, some cases more extreme than others.

4. *Certain Things Open the Door to Demonic Influence*

So far, we have covered some foundational truths about the work of evil spirits and the reality and prevalence of demonic influence. We now come to an important question: *how do evil spirits gain access to people's lives in the first place?* The following passage gives us some insight into how evil spirits operate.

When an unclean spirit goes out of a man, he goes through dry places, seeking rest, and finds none. Then he says, "I will return to my house from which I came." And when he comes, he finds it empty, swept, and put in order. Then he goes and takes with him seven other spirits more wicked than himself, and they enter and dwell there; and the last state of that man is worse than the first... (Matthew 12:43-45).

From this passage we learn that demons have some form of intelligence—the ability to think, reason, and make decisions. The unclean spirit that Jesus mentions has a thought process, speaks, and uses its will to act. We can see that demons work together in groups and that some are more wicked than others. We learn that once we are delivered, we must replace what was cast out by being filled with the Holy Spirit and the truth of God's Word. We must be ready to continue to resist the devil, as evil spirits may try to regain access. This should not make us afraid, but aware of our need to be vigilant.

Notice what the unclean spirit says about the person from whom it was cast out: "I will return to *my house*." Demons seek a body to dwell in, and without one they are homeless and restless. Just as the Holy Spirit dwells inside of believers and desires to express His nature through us, evil spirits seek a person through whom they can live and express their wickedness and perversion. To the spiritual world, the human body is considered a house. This is a significant truth for understanding the ministry of deliverance, and it comes into play as we consider how demons gain access to a person. Demons cannot simply inhabit, influence, or torment whomever they please. In order to gain access into a person's life there must be an open door through which to enter. Just as you enter a house through the door, there are various doors that can be opened up to give evil spirits entrance.

It is important to recognize how evil spirits gain access to people's lives so that we can know how to shut the door on the devil. We want to be able to get free, resist the enemy's schemes, and walk in the fullness of our freedom. Throughout the following chapters, we will cover various open doors in more detail. But I want to summarize some of these access points here.

A key principle to understand is that *agreement* with the devil gives *access* to the devil. "What agreement has the temple of God with idols?" (2 Corinthians 6:16). There is no agreement between the temple of God and idols, and there should be no agreement between believers and the devil. If we violate this principle by coming into alignment with satan, we can open the door to evil spirits. One of the ways that we can come into agreement with the devil is through walking in ongoing, unrepentant sin.

Sin is not only rebellion against God, it is agreement with satan. When Adam and Eve first sinned in the Garden of Eden, they not only disobeyed God, they agreed with the serpent. When we embrace and justify sin instead of bringing sin into the light and truly repenting of it, we are living in agreement with the devil and give him a right to an area of our lives. A perfect example of this is Paul's teaching on anger. Ephesians 4:26-27 says, "'Be angry, and do not sin': do not let the sun go down on your wrath, nor give place to the devil." It is possible to be angry without sinning, but if you let your anger fester it can turn into sin. At this point you "give place to the devil." Walking in ongoing unrepentant sin gives the devil a place in our lives.

As followers of Jesus, we may struggle with sin and temptation at times, but we are never to come into agreement with sin and we need not be bound by it. There is a big difference between the person who stumbles into sin and yet walks in quick repentance and the person who embraces sin and no longer sees the need to stand against it. If you are justifying, minimizing, or hiding sin in the dark, you are giving the kingdom of darkness access. We must come clean before the Lord and have a heart that truly desires to walk in holiness. The longer a person walks in agreement with the enemy by embracing sin in their life, the more the door is opened for evil spirits to influence them.

Another way that we can come into agreement with the devil is by believing his lies. Just as knowing the truth will set us free, believing a lie will create a bondage. The Bible says that satan is the "father of lies" (see John 8:44). He is always whispering lies about the character of God, the Word of God, our identity in Christ, and anything else that suits his purposes. The fact that the devil is a liar does not open the door to him; but if we believe his lies we have agreed with him, and again, this gives him a point of access. I have seen cases where a demonic spirit was present to reinforce a specific lie of the enemy. In one instance, a young man needed deliverance from a demon after he had believed the lie that he had committed the unpardonable sin and could not be forgiven.

Along with places of agreement, evil spirits will also look for *moments of weakness* as an access point. In First Peter 5:8 we are told that the devil "walks about like a roaring lion, seeking whom he may devour." He is actively searching for people to prey on. He is looking for open doors into our lives, and one of the places he looks is moments of weakness. He seeks to take advantage of times when our guard is down or when we are at a place of vulnerability. This can often happen when we go through a traumatic experience or are the victim of abuse.

When a person endures abuse—physical, verbal, sexual, emotional, or otherwise—it creates a scenario where the one being abused is susceptible to becoming demonized. In these cases, it is not their own sin but the sin of somebody else that can open the door. This does not seem fair at all; but who said that the devil plays fair? He takes advantage of the moment of weakness that trauma establishes and uses it to slip into a person's life. In walking with those who have been abused,

I have seen instances in which getting delivered from evil spirits was an important part of the healing process.

Other traumatic events can create a moment of weakness that the enemy exploits. Examples could include going through a terrible relational betrayal or devastating divorce, having a death in the family, fighting through a terminal illness, witnessing or being the victim of a violent crime, or being in a serious accident.

The enemy also seeks to take advantage of children, who don't have the mental and spiritual defenses to guard against such attacks. When a child is exposed to something dark, horrific, or sinful, it can cause an access point for evil spirits. A child who is terrified by a horror movie could become susceptible to a spirit of fear. A young person who gets exposed to pornography can be targeted by unclean spirits of perversion and sexual sin. When children witness violence or fighting in the home, it can welcome evil spirits. When a child endures rejection, neglect, or abandonment, it can give the enemy a place to try to enter.

Another general category of open doors is what is sometimes referred to as *legal rights*. These are related to violations of God's laws and principles that give the devil permission to have ground in a person's life. An example of this type of open door is unforgiveness. In Matthew 18, Jesus tells a parable about the importance forgiveness. When the servant of a king is forgiven his very large debt but refuses to forgive his fellow servant a much smaller debt, the king becomes angry. Here is how Jesus describes it: "And his master was angry, and delivered him to the torturers until he should pay all that was due to him" (Matthew 18:34). He goes on to make a sobering statement: "So My heavenly Father also will do to you if each of you, from his heart, does not forgive his brother his trespasses" (Matthew 18:35). Notice that the unforgiving servant was delivered to the torturers by the king.

It is not God's will for us to be in demonic torment. But ongoing unforgiveness gives the devil God-given permission to torment you. It puts you in a spiritual prison to be afflicted by spiritual "torturers." It gives the enemy a legal right in the eyes of God. The devil and his demons see unforgiveness in the life of a believer as a perfect point of access, because they have biblical basis to enter. Many people are set free from torment, including physical sickness, when they forgive the ones who have hurt them and sinned against them. (In a later chapter, I will address some common misunderstandings about forgiveness, and show that we can extend forgiveness while maintaining necessary boundaries with abusive or destructive individuals.)

Another example of a legal right for the enemy to enter is any involvement in idolatry or the occult. The Bible is clear that the worship of idols is actually demon worship (see 1 Corinthians 10:19-20). And involvement in the occult is strictly forbidden throughout the Scriptures. The occult refers to hidden or secret supernatural arts. It is a broad topic and there is much that could be said about it. But any attempt to gain supernatural power or knowledge apart from the one true living God is a dangerous practice. When we cross into the enemy's territory through dabbling in the occult, embracing New Age practices, or worshiping idols, we are giving evil spirits access to our lives. (See Deuteronomy 18:9-14 for some examples of occult practices.)

Finally, generational sin, or the "sins of the fathers," can give the enemy a legal point of access. This is sometimes referred to as a generational curse where the sins of previous generations are "visited upon" the children (see Exodus 20:5). Just as we receive an inheritance from our parents in regard to our physical traits, we also receive a spiritual inheritance that can include both blessings and curses. These are not just superstitious beliefs but very real forces at work. You can often look at family lines and see cycles of specific sinful tendencies, abusive behavior, addiction, or other harmful patterns. Sometimes demonic spirits are involved to reinforce these sinful and destructive inclinations, carrying them down the generational line.

Again, we will cover more about these and other demonic access points throughout the remainder of this book. And you can always go to Appendix 1 for a succinct list of common open doors to demonic influence.

5. Christians Can Be Under Demonic Influence

The question of whether or not a genuine Christian can have a demon is probably the most controversial aspect of the ministry of deliverance. The answer to this question has far-reaching implications, because it dramatically impacts how we view the various problems that Christians are dealing with. There is no doubt that many Christians are struggling with a wide range of issues. Tormenting fears, bondage to sin, deep depression, and mental health issues are just a few of the problems that many believers are dealing with today. What if demonic influence is a factor or even the root cause of some of these issues? If it is believed that a Christian cannot have a demon, then it will not be dealt with from the perspective of deliverance from an evil spirit and therefore no true or lasting freedom will be achieved.

Before God opened my eyes to the truth about deliverance and led me into this ministry, I believed that a Christian could not have a demon. In fact, many believers have strong a strong conviction about this, as if we should not even consider the possibility of a Christian needing deliverance. After all, how can the Holy Spirit and an evil spirit dwell in the same body? How can a demon inhabit God's temple? This is the primary argument for those who believe that a Christian cannot have a demon, and at a glance it appears to be sound reasoning. But does it really line up with Scripture? Let's take this same logic and apply it to the temple in the Old Testament.

Israel's history is plagued with idolatry, and at times idols were even brought into the temple of God. For instance, the Bible says this about King Manasseh: "He even set a carved image, the idol which he had made, in the house of God" (2 Chronicles 33:7). This is significant to our discussion because there is a direct correlation between idols and demons. Consider Psalm 106:36-38:

*They served their **idols**,*

Which became a snare to them.

They even sacrificed their sons

*And their daughters to **demons**,*

And shed innocent blood,

The blood of their sons and daughters,

*Whom they sacrificed to the **idols** of Canaan;*

And the land was polluted with blood.

Paul also makes this same connection between idols and demons in First Corinthians 10:19-20: "What am I saying then? That an idol is anything, or what is offered to idols is anything? Rather, that the things which the Gentiles sacrifice they sacrifice to demons and not to God, and I do not want you to have fellowship with demons." These two passages make it clear that a sacrifice made to an idol is actually a sacrifice made to a demon.

Why am I emphasizing this point? Because it shows that it is possible to bring demons into the temple of God. When King Manasseh brought his idols into God's house, he was allowing demons entrance. Not only did he bring idols into the temple, he also built altars there in order to sacrifice to these false gods (see 2 Chronicles 33:4). As we have just seen, sacrificing to an idol is the equivalent of sacrificing to a demon. There is a biblical precedent for demons inhabiting the house of God, and if it could happen in the Old Testament temple why could it not happen in the New Testament temple, the body of a believer?

The belief that a Christian cannot have a demon is based to a large degree on a misunderstanding of what it means to have a demon.

To have a demon does not mean that you are *possessed* by a demon. Unfortunately, many English translations of the Bible use the term "demon-possessed" to describe a person in need of deliverance. For example, Matthew 8:16 says, "When evening had come, they brought to Him *many who were demon-possessed*. And He cast out the spirits with a word, and healed all who were sick." The Greek word that is translated "demon-possessed" in the above passage is *daimonizomai*, which is a commonly used term to describe the influence of demons in the New Testament. A more accurate translation of this word would be "to have a demon," to be "influenced by a demon," or to be "demonized."

This is an important distinction to make. The word "possessed" denotes total ownership. This would imply that the person no longer has any control of their actions or words and that the demon is totally in charge. But this is not the case, especially for believers. A Christian cannot be owned or possessed by a demon, but a demon can be present and be influencing their life.

The belief that a Christian cannot have a demon is also based on a misunderstanding of what it means to be the temple of the Holy Spirit. To say that being the temple of the Holy Spirit automatically takes away the possibility of having a demon is an argument that is based more on human logic than biblical fact. Using this same logic, you would also have to conclude that it is impossible for a believer to sin or ever have an evil thought. For how can sin—which is contrary to God's nature—be in His temple? How can evil thoughts be in the mind of a believer, when we have the mind of Christ (see 1 Corinthians 2:16)? Yet we know that believers do stumble into sin and that they can and do have evil thoughts at times. The same people who argue that a Christian cannot have a demon would never argue that it is impossible for a Christian to sin or have a dark thought. This is inconsistent logic.

It is clear that there is no agreement between the temple of God and idols (see 2 Corinthians 6:16). Yet idols were brought into God's temple. In the same way, evil spirits do not belong in God's house, but that does not mean that it is impossible for them to be there. We seem to have the idea that the temple was like a one-room box, and if God was in it, nothing evil could be present. But the temple had three main areas as well as many rooms, chambers, and other quarters. God's manifest presence was in the Holy of Holies, but not necessarily the rest of the temple. Using this comparison, it is my belief that a demon cannot inhabit the spirit of a born-again believer (where the Holy Spirit dwells), but that it is possible for one to occupy a place in the flesh or the soul (mind, will, and emotions).

I want to say clearly that not all problems and struggles that Christians face are caused by demons. But it is also true that many believers *do* have problems caused, at least in part, by demons. And if we do not deal with the demonic element, they will never experience the fullness of freedom that Christ purchased for them on the cross.

Repairing the House

Earlier in this chapter we saw that to the spiritual world, the human body is considered a house. When a person becomes a believer, they are redeemed from the kingdom of darkness and the devil's hand. God is now the owner of the house and He comes to dwell inside. But the previous owner did not treat the house very well, and there is a need for some renovation and remodeling. Perhaps there are also a few rooms that are filled with junk and are in need of cleansing. These rooms represent different aspects of the person's emotions, mind, or flesh that have become influenced by evil spirits. Deliverance is the process of shining the light on these areas and cleaning these rooms so that the whole house can be clean. Just because a person comes to

Christ, it does not mean that all of these areas are automatically dealt with and cleaned out at once.

When God redeems us, He purchases "the house" as is. He doesn't wait for us to get all cleaned up first. We turn to Him in genuine repentance and sincere faith, and He saves us and comes to dwell on the inside. There is then some ongoing sanctification that needs to occur after conversion, and part of that process may include freedom from evil spirits. Deliverance is simply enforcing the finished work of Jesus so that what was accomplished on the cross becomes a greater reality in our experience. In this way, deliverance can be a part of the process of renewal and sanctification.

Perhaps as you read through this chapter, you have realized that there are some doors that have opened you up to the influence of evil spirits. Ask the Holy Spirit to continue to lead you and show you if there is anything else that needs to be remembered or brought into the light. Trust Him to walk you through deliverance and give you peace. There is no need to be afraid. Thankfully, you can close every door and receive deliverance because of what Jesus has done for us. In this chapter, we covered five foundational truths about demonic influence, but in the next chapter we will cover another essential truth: In Christ, we have authority over evil spirits.

| 3 |

POWER AND AUTHORITY
OVER DEMONS

W hen it comes to the topics of spiritual warfare and deliverance, we must keep things in the proper perspective. On the one hand, we must not be ignorant of the devil's schemes. But on the other hand, we must not become fearful, paranoid, or overly focused on the kingdom of darkness. There is a healthy balance in how we walk this out. Our posture toward the demonic realm should be that we are aware but not afraid and familiar but not fascinated. Keeping our focus on Jesus is of paramount importance.

Stay Focused on Jesus

The demonic realm is real, and spiritual warfare is a part of our journey. We must not be unaware of the works of the enemy and our need to overcome them, but we must keep intimacy with God as the highest priority. We must be vigilant to stand firm against the kingdom of darkness and open and ready to receive deliverance when it is needed, without becoming paranoid or afraid of evil spirits. It is not always easy to walk in a healthy balance in these matters, but with the help of the Holy Spirit and instruction of the Scriptures we can achieve this. James 4:7-8 gives us some great wisdom in this regard: "Therefore submit to God. Resist the devil and he will flee from you. Draw near to God and He will draw near to you." Notice that two out of the three commands are God-focused while one is focused on resisting the devil. That is a good ratio. We focus on submitting to God, drawing near to Him in relationship, and fulfilling our purpose in His kingdom; all the while ready to resist the devil so that he will flee.

When Jesus called His twelve disciples, He purposed to equip and send them to advance the Kingdom of God and destroy the works of the devil. But He established the priority of relationship with Him first. We can see this outlined in Mark 3:13-15:

> *And He went up on the mountain and called to Him those He Himself wanted. And they came to Him. Then He appointed twelve, **that they might be with Him** and that He might send them out to preach, and to have power to heal sicknesses and to cast out demons.*

Jesus had a clear mission for His disciples. They would be sent out as His representatives and would fulfill specific tasks such as preaching, healing the sick, and casting out demons. But before they were called to *do*, they were called to *be*. Specifically, they were called to *be with Him*. They were called to relationship first and assignment second. The assignment flowed out of the relationship. Both are essential, but if we place the task above the relationship, we are out of order and will get off track.

Just like the disciples' first calling was to be with Jesus, our first priority is to be with God and know Him more. As we seek to be set free from captivity and to set others free, it is important to keep our relationship with God as the primary focus. Yes, it is vital to know the biblical basics of spiritual warfare and deliverance. It is important to examine yourself under the guidance of the Holy Spirit to discern whether there are any areas where you are in need of deliverance. But at the same time, I would caution you not to become too introspective or preoccupied with trying to figure it all out. One of the keys to staying on track and avoiding excesses is to keep our relationship with God central in our lives. Trust Him to show you what you need to know. Ask the Holy Spirit to guide you, even as you read this book.

We Can't Ignore Demons

I must reiterate that while we must keep our focus on Jesus and on our relationship with God, this does *not* mean that we can simply ignore demons. The apostle Paul specifically stated that we are not to be ignorant of the devil's devices, lest he take advantage of us (see 2 Corinthians 2:11).

There seems to be an increasing number of believers who are taking an approach to the devil that is totally foreign to the New Testament. The thought process goes something like this: because Jesus already defeated satan through His death and resurrection, we can pretty much ignore him now. While the premise is true, the conclusion is very false. It might seem nice to pretend like the devil doesn't exist or we never have to deal with demons, but this is not the reality of the world in which we live. It would go against the example of Jesus, the commission He has given the Church, and the clear teachings of the New Testament. The Bible says to *resist* the devil and he will flee, not to *ignore* the devil and he will flee (see James 4:7).

Jesus called the twelve disciples to spend time with Him, but then He later sent them out to cast out unclean spirits:

> *And he called the twelve and began to send them out two by two, and gave them authority over the unclean spirits. ... And they cast out many demons and anointed with oil many who were sick and healed them* (Mark 6:7,13 ESV).

Again, the mindset of ignoring the devil and demons sounds pleasant. Who wants to deal with dark spirits? But there is a major problem with this belief system: *the New Testament paints a drastically different picture.* While showing that the devil has been defeated by the work of Christ, it also portrays an ongoing conflict with the kingdom of darkness until the final judgment. At a glance this might seem like a contradiction, but it is the clear teaching of Scripture. The verdict is in—the devil has been defeated. But the judgment has not been fully executed yet, and until that time we will have spiritual conflict. Casting out demons and setting captives free is enforcing the finished work that Jesus has already paid the price for. There is a battle, but we fight *from* victory, *not* for victory.

We Don't Need to Be Afraid of Demons

Just as we must not ignore the devil or his demons, we must also not be afraid of them. When God first began to lead me into deliverance ministry, the prospect of casting out an evil spirit made me scared. I knew in my mind that Jesus had all authority. *But me? Casting demons? Surely not!* Now that I have been involved with deliverance for many years, I understand that there is no need to be afraid of evil spirits.

Why is there a tendency to be afraid of evil spirits? There could be a variety of reasons:

- Maybe we have seen Hollywood portrayals of wild demonic possession, which always seem to glorify the power of satan and minimize the power of God.

- Perhaps we have been exposed to deliverance ministry that was done in a wild, chaotic way or our only experience with deliverance has been unbiblical extremes.

- Perhaps the enemy himself is projecting fear on us, to keep us away from this topic so he won't be exposed.

- We might not have a firm grasp on the victory of Jesus or be rooted in the fact that we have been given authority over demons in His name.

The truth is, we do not need to be afraid of evil spirits. "For God has not given us a spirit of fear, but of power and of love and of a sound mind" (2 Timothy 1:7). Demons want us to be afraid of them so that we will feel intimidated at the prospect of receiving deliverance or ministering deliverance to others. This is just one of their schemes to try to keep us in the chains of oppression, torment, bondage, and affliction.

Jesus paid the price for our deliverance and He has given us authority over evil spirits. Consider the following verses:

Then He called His twelve disciples together and gave them power and authority over all demons... (Luke 9:1).

Then the seventy returned with joy, saying, "Lord, even the demons are subject to us in Your name." And He said to them, "I saw Satan fall like lightning from heaven. Behold, I give you the authority to trample on serpents and scorpions, and over all the power of the enemy, and nothing shall by any means hurt you. Nevertheless do not rejoice in this, that the spirits are subject to you, but rather rejoice because your names are written in heaven" (Luke 10:17-20).

And these signs will follow those who believe: In My name they will cast out demons… (Mark 16:17).

Here is the truth about our spiritual authority: *in the name of Jesus, demons are subject to us.* While Jesus reminded His followers to take more joy in the fact that their names were registered in Heaven, He also confirmed their position of spiritual authority over demons. We do not need to be afraid to learn about deliverance, receive deliverance, or cast evil spirits out of others. We should not be arrogant about our authority over demons, but we must embrace it and walk in it with confidence and boldness. Evil spirits want you to be afraid of them, but the truth is that they are terrified of Christ in you! So don't let fear of the enemy cause you to remain in darkness or oppression. Don't be intimidated by evil spirits or afraid of the topic of deliverance. Use wisdom, walk in humility, and exercise discernment; but do not allow fear to paralyze you or keep you from freedom.

Power and Authority over Demons

When Jesus sent out His disciples to preach and minister, He specifically gave them *power* and *authority* over demons. Let's read Luke 9:1 again: "Then He called His twelve disciples together and gave them power and authority over all demons." The terms *authority* and *power* are related, but they each carry a unique meaning and purpose. Let's break down these two words, noting their differences and how they relate to casting out demons and setting captives free.

1. Authority

The word *authority* implies a legal right to perform a task. In other words, the disciples were *authorized* to cast out demons. When Jesus commissioned them to preach the Gospel, heal the sick, and cast out demons, He gave them the necessary authority to carry out these works. As an example, a police officer has been authorized by the government to enforce the law, and therefore can pull over a person who is speeding and issue them a ticket. If I were to see someone speeding, I could not legally try to pull them over because I have not been authorized to do so. In the same way that police officers are authorized to enforce the law, we as believers have been authorized to enforce the victory that was won in the finished work of Jesus over the powers of darkness.

After His death and resurrection, Jesus spoke the following words before ascending to Heaven, "All authority has been given to Me in heaven and on earth" (Matthew 28:18). He then gave the disciples what is known as the Great Commission, sending them into the world to make disciples of all nations. Although all authority belongs to Jesus, He has delegated that authority to His followers who are to use it to advance His Kingdom. Our authority comes from being in Christ, the One who possesses all authority.

Our authority to cast out demons is also rooted in God's Word. In other words, we have authority over evil spirits simply because God has said that we do. Consider again these verses:

> *And these signs will follow those who believe: In My name they will cast out demons...* (Mark 16:17).
> *Behold, I give you the authority to trample on serpents and scorpions, and over all the power of the enemy, and nothing shall by any means hurt you* (Luke 10:19).

These passages declare the authority of the believer over evil spirits, giving us the right to command demons to come out of people. When we exercise this authority over demons, we must do so in the name of Jesus. Notice that the Mark 16:17 passage quoted above says, "In *My name* they will cast out demons." Our authority is not of ourselves but in Him and from Him, who is the Source of all authority. When we exercise authority over demons, it is important that we speak with absolute faith in the power of the Word of God and the name of Jesus.

Demons recognize the authority of God's Word and the power of the name of Jesus. They know that they must obey the servants of the living God, even if they try to resist at times. We can be confident in our authority to cast out evil spirits and resist the devil. But along with authority, we must also walk in power.

2. Power

While authority relates to the legal right to perform a task, power refers to the *ability* to perform it. As an illustration, suppose that you would like to have a tree removed from your yard. You call a tree removal company and they come to your house. A random person could not legally come into your yard and remove one of your trees; that would be trespassing. But the tree removal company can perform this task because you have authorized them to do so. Now suppose that the person from the tree removal company attempts to uproot the tree using only his bare hands. He tries and tries to pull it out, but the tree will not budge. He has all the authority in the world to remove the tree, but what he lacks is power. The proper equipment and machinery would give him the ability he needs to easily remove the tree from your yard.

In the same way, we have authority to cast out demons, but we also need power in order to set captives free. This power comes to us as we are anointed with and empowered by the Holy Spirit. It was the anointing of the Holy Spirit that empowered Jesus to fulfill His mission. Notice this emphasis in the opening lines of Luke 4:18:

> *The Spirit of the Lord is upon Me,*
> *Because He has anointed Me*

To preach the gospel to the poor;
He has sent Me to heal the brokenhearted,
To proclaim liberty to the captives
And recovery of sight to the blind,
To set at liberty those who are oppressed.

It was the Holy Spirit resting upon Him who gave Jesus the power to set the captives free. Though He never ceased to be God, He was also fully man and functioned in His ministry as a man empowered by the Spirit. He even said that He cast out demons "by the Spirit of God" (Matthew 12:28). Peter described the ministry of Jesus like this: "God anointed Jesus of Nazareth with the Holy Spirit and with power, who went about doing good and healing all who were oppressed by the devil, for God was with Him" (Acts 10:38). How much more do we need the power of the Holy Spirit!

When the Power of God Comes

A personal example comes to mind to illustrate the difference between authority and power and our need for the Holy Spirit's anointing. One evening my wife and I were praying for a young lady to receive deliverance from demons but were not making much progress. She had prayed through a prayer to close every door of demonic access, and I began to command the demons to leave. The spirits were obviously being stirred up and began to manifest. But even though I continued to make commands, the demons would not leave. After about 15 minutes of this, I asked her to stand up and I asked the Holy Spirit to come and minister to her. All of a sudden, she fell backward under the power of God and the demons began to come out one by one with little or no effort on my part. Supernatural discernment was given to me and the spirits were leaving faster than I could command them. I

45

had the authority all along, but when the power of the Holy Spirit fell, deliverance happened very quickly without any struggle.

One of the specific ways that the power of the Holy Spirit can be released in deliverance ministry is through His supernatural gifts. For example, the gift of discerning spirits can expose the presence and name of a specific evil spirit. A word of knowledge can pinpoint a root cause that needs to be dealt with, such as unforgiveness or occult activity. The gift of faith can rise up in a person and cause them to have unusual boldness and confidence in confronting and casting out a demon. The gifts of the Holy Spirit can be powerful weapons to help the process of deliverance and bring breakthrough.

If we are to be effective in walking in freedom and setting captives free, we need to be filled with the Holy Spirit. Being indwelt by the Holy Spirit at salvation is not the same as being empowered by the Holy Spirit. This empowerment starts by receiving the baptism of the Holy Spirit that Jesus promised and continues as we live a lifestyle of being continually filled. As we walk in more of the Holy Spirit's power, we will see deliverances happen with less struggle. It will take less time, be more thorough, and bring greater freedom to those in need. Deliverance can certainly be progressive in nature, with the Lord putting His finger on specific areas over a period of time. But when Jesus ministered, the man with the legion of demons was fully delivered and restored in his mind through one encounter. I believe we will see greater effectiveness as we cry out for and receive a greater anointing from the Holy Spirit.

If you want an increase of the power of the Holy Spirit in your life, I would suggest you do two things: first, spend time waiting on the Lord in prayer, asking specifically for the power of the Holy Spirit. Second, receive the laying on of hands from those who are already walking in a greater measure of the genuine power of God than you. As you seek for more, remember that the power of the Holy Spirit does not come upon us for our own sake, but for the glory of God and the benefit of others. Let the Lord purify your motives as you ask for an increase of His power.

Using Spiritual Weapons

Exercising authority and power over demons is the basic way that deliverance happens. The primary way to remove a demon is to speak directly to it, commanding it to come out in the name of Jesus. But God has also given us some spiritual weapons that we can employ when confronting powers of darkness. These can aid the process of deliverance and bring needed breakthrough. We have supernatural weapons that we can use to demolish the enemy's strongholds and set captives free.

The following is a list of some items in our spiritual arsenal. These should not be used in a formulaic or ritualistic way, but as the Holy Spirit leads.

1. *The Blood of Jesus*

The Bible says that we overcome satan by the blood of the Lamb (see Revelation 12:11). It is because of the blood of Jesus that we are redeemed from the hand of the devil. It is by the blood that we are delivered from the dominion of darkness and brought into the Kingdom of light. It is through the blood that we are forgiven and justified, removing the enemy's claim on us. The finished work of Jesus in His death, resurrection, and ascension is the basis for everything we receive from God. Declaring and claiming the power of the blood of Jesus over ourselves or those seeking freedom from captivity can be an effective weapon in spiritual battle. Demons hate the mention of the blood of Christ!

2. *The Word of God*

When receiving or ministering deliverance, proclaiming Scriptures can be a powerful weapon of warfare. Jesus quoted the Word of God when He faced the devil in the wilderness. The apostle Paul called the Word of God the "sword of the Spirit" (Ephesians 6:17). It is a weapon to be used in spiritual warfare. Demons recognize the Word of God and know that it is the truth. They know that they are subject to us in the name of Jesus and that God's Word has power over them. Declaring verses that affirm the devil's defeat and the authority of believers over demons can be a powerful tool in dislodging demons.

3. *Speaking in Tongues*

I have found that speaking in tongues can be effective when driving out demons. This is not surprising, as the apostle Paul states that praying in the Spirit is linked with spiritual warfare (see Ephesians 6:18). Several years ago, I was praying over a person for deliverance and there seemed to be a standstill. I began to speak in tongues and it had an immediate effect, causing demons to manifest and be expelled. I have now seen similar occurrences happen many times. If you speak in tongues, be sensitive to the Holy Spirit about when it might be good to exercise this gift during deliverance.

4. *Intercessory Prayer*

Sometimes it is good to pause during a deliverance session and cry out to God in the name of Jesus. In these moments, we shift from exercising authority over demons to interceding for the person. Ask God to send angels to help in the battle. Call out in prayer for complete deliverance. It is also good to have the one being prayed for call out to Jesus. The Bible says, "Whoever calls on the name of the Lord will be delivered" (Joel 2:32 NASB). Intercessory prayer can release breakthrough and freedom as God steps in.

5. Anointing with Oil

Mark 6:13 says, "And they cast out many demons, and anointed with oil many who were sick, and healed them." I will sometimes anoint people with oil when I pray for deliverance. There is nothing magical in the oil, but it is a symbol of the presence of the Holy Spirit, and God can use it as a means of releasing His power. I have seen demons cause a person to try to avoid being anointed with oil—they don't like it! Have some anointing oil ready when you are praying for deliverance and be sensitive to the Lord about if and when to use it. Ask for the anointing of the Spirit to break every yoke of oppression and bondage (see Isaiah 10:27).

The Role of Angels

Not only do we have spiritual weapons to aid us in battle, we also have spiritual warriors on our side. While the topic of this book is demons and deliverance from their influence, let's not forget that the spiritual realm is not relegated to darkness only. God has hosts of angels that are sent into the world to do His work, fulfill His commands, and minister to His people. In fact, the writer of Hebrews says that God's Kingdom has an "innumerable company of angels" (Hebrews 12:22). These angels are described as "ministering spirits sent forth to minister for those who will inherit salvation" (Hebrews 1:14).

Angels are spiritual beings that are part of God's heavenly Kingdom. There are hundreds of references to angels in the Bible, and they play a prominent role throughout both the Old and New Testaments. It is beyond the scope of this book to do an exhaustive biblical study on the ministry of angels and the many facets of their work in the earth. But I want to look briefly at how angels can be involved in helping to bring deliverance.

The angel of the Lord encamps all around those who fear Him, and delivers them (Psalm 34:7).

For He shall give His angels charge over you,

To keep you in all your ways.

In their hands they shall bear you up,

Lest you dash your foot against a stone.

You shall tread upon the lion and the cobra,

The young lion and the serpent you shall

trample underfoot (Psalm 91:11-13).

As I have studied Scripture and walked in practical experience, I have come to appreciate the importance of angels in general and in deliverance specifically. God doesn't need to use angels to accomplish His purposes, but it appears that He often chooses to. While it would be foolish to give them too much attention or focus, it would also be foolish to ignore their role in the Kingdom of God. When I minister deliverance in large group settings or personal prayer ministry, I make it a point to ask the Father to send His angels to assist in the ministry. Multiple people who operate in the gift of discerning of spirits have reported seeing or otherwise discerning the presence of angels in such times.

Once I was praying for a woman for deliverance, and whenever a demon would manifest there was a sharp pain in her back. At one point in the prayer session I asked God to send angels to minister to her, and when I did, she felt a sensation on her back and the pain went away. The next morning, I happened to be reading Matthew 4 and verse 11 stood out to me: "Then the devil left Him, and behold, angels came and ministered to Him." Note that Jesus Himself was ministered to by angels. I observed that it was in the context of spiritual conflict that the angels came to His assistance and remembered the prayer ministry session from the night before.

When you are receiving or ministering deliverance, ask God to send angels on assignment to help bring breakthrough and deliverance. I don't believe we are to command angels directly, but we can petition the Father to release them to our aid. They are agents of Heaven who can help break demonic chains and do battle in the spiritual realm.

Prayer for Authority and Power

As we come to the close of this chapter, I encourage you to take some time in a quiet place to pray. Use the words below, and add your own words as well. Once you have prayed, take time to quietly wait on the Lord in expectation for the Holy Spirit to come upon you and fill you afresh.

Heavenly Father, I come to You in the name of Jesus. I thank You for the gift of salvation and the finished work of Christ on the cross. I thank You that through the blood of Jesus, I am forgiven and cleansed from all unrighteousness. I thank You that the devil is defeated and You are victorious.

Right now, I step into a greater place of faith and Kingdom authority. I reject all fear of the devil or evil spirits and recognize that You have given me authority over demons in the name of Jesus. As I submit my life to You, I can resist the devil and he will flee. I trust Your Word and receive this authority now, in Jesus' name.

I thank You for the gift of the Holy Spirit. I welcome the Holy Spirit in my life to fill me, lead me, and empower me in fresh ways. Let Your Spirit lead me into all truth, guide me into greater freedom, and anoint me to set captives free! In Jesus' name, amen.

| 4 |

HOW TO RECEIVE DELIVERANCE

I hope that as you've read the last few chapters, you are gaining more insight into the reality of demonic influence and the ministry of deliverance. Jesus came to bring freedom, and He has not changed. He is "the same yesterday, today, and forever" (Hebrews 13:8). He is still in the business of healing broken hearts and setting captives free.

The next several chapters will include teachings, testimonies, and prayers for how to break free from the chains of various types of demonic influence. But before we move forward into these specific areas, I want to outline some foundational truths and keys for receiving deliverance in this chapter. This will help to keep things in a good perspective and prepare your heart to receive freedom.

Deliverance Can Be Progressive

Having led thousands of people through deliverance prayers in both personal and group settings, I have come to see that there are some general principles that can be applied to most situations. But I have also learned that every situation is unique and requires the wisdom and guidance of the Holy Spirit. There have been many times when deliverance happened quickly and easily, and other cases in which it was more of a struggle to gain breakthrough. There have been some occasions when little to no progress was made. I don't always know the answer to why some cases are harder than others, but I believe that there are at least three factors involved in any given ministry situation.

The first factor is the "God factor." What is He putting His finger on and how is He sovereignly moving? Are there certain areas that He is highlighting first in the person's process of restoration and deliverance? A second factor is the spiritual condition of the one who is receiving ministry. What degree of demonic influence are they under? Are they submitted to God and willing to repent where needed? Are they walking in forgiveness toward those who have hurt or sinned against them? Are they willing to close every door and are they truly desiring freedom? The third factor is the anointing and grace on the person who is ministering. Are they walking in faith and authority? Is the Holy Spirit's anointing upon them? What spiritual gifts flow through them? Any one of these three factors can impact the outcome and effectiveness of a time of ministry for deliverance.

I have also observed that it is not uncommon for deliverance to happen in a progressive way. If a person needs deliverance in multiple areas, sometimes God will deal with one or two areas at one time and then move on to other areas at a later time. While it is certainly God's desire for His children to walk in total freedom, He may move in a specific way in a given prayer session or lead a person through full deliverance progressively over the course of time. We can see a parallel in how the Lord drove out the enemy nations from the Promised Land so that the children of Israel would inherit it step by step instead of all at once.

I will not drive them out from before you in one year, lest the land become desolate and the beasts of the field become too numerous for you. Little by little I will drive them out from before you, until you have increased, and you inherit the land (Exodus 23:29-30).

Sometimes, it might be best for a person to receive deliverance in stages so that they can be established in one area of freedom before moving on to the next. If you end up needing multiple prayer sessions to get total freedom, that is totally fine. What is important is to keep moving forward and taking more ground. I often remind people that Jesus is their Deliverer and that He will lead them in their process of freedom and restoration. Every situation is case by case, and we must rely on the Holy Spirit and keep our eyes on Jesus.

There is a balance in all of this. While deliverance can be progressive in nature, I also believe that as we receive a greater anointing of the Holy Spirit and power, we will see deliverance happen more quickly and thoroughly. After all, in one encounter with Jesus, the man with the legion of demons was completely set free and healed in his mind (see Mark 5:1-20). But just because we are not functioning at the level of Jesus doesn't mean we should become discouraged. Let's use what we have, while contending to walk in a greater authority, grace, and power to set captives free.

Three Keys for Receiving Deliverance

If you are in need of freedom from demonic influence, I want to guide you through some practical points that will help aid the process. There is no exact formula for deliverance, but there are some foundational principles that apply to the majority of situations. I often teach that there are three basic keys for deliverance:

1. Discerning the presence of evil spirits

2. Discovering and closing any open doors

3. Driving out the evil spirits

These keys can be applied when you are receiving deliverance for yourself or when you are ministering it to others. They serve as a basic track to follow as you seek the Holy Spirit's wisdom and direction. Let's take a look at each of these below.

Key 1: Discerning the Presence of Evil Spirits

How do you know when an evil spirit is at work in your life? How do you know when an area of bondage involves demonic influence or is simply the flesh? How can you tell if a sickness or physical affliction is the result of natural causes or a spirit of infirmity? How can you determine whether the torment in your mind is coming from an evil spirit or is physiological in nature? These are all very good questions. It is important to understand that not every problem is caused by a demon. It is also important to be aware that many problems *are* caused by demons and that it is not always obvious to the natural eye when a demon is involved. This is why we need to cultivate spiritual discernment.

Discerning an evil spirit is like turning the lights on in a dark basement to find that a deadly serpent is hiding in the corner. Until the lights were turned on you couldn't recognize the presence of this harmful intruder in your home, but it was there nonetheless. Once revealed, the serpent can be effectively dealt with. In the same way, for evil spirits to be *expelled* they must first be *exposed*. When they are brought into the light they can be addressed and cast out. But as long as they remain hidden and undetected, they can continue their destructive work in and through the person in whom they dwell. Discerning the presence of evil spirits can happen in different ways, and we can grow in our discernment through study, practical experience, and walking in the Holy Spirit. When I teach on discerning evil spirits, I normally mention three primary ways this happens: a *demonic manifestation, supernatural revelation from the Holy Spirit,* and what I would call *natural discernment.* I will cover these in the following pages.

1. A Demonic Manifestation

One of the ways that evil spirits can be discerned is when there is a demonic manifestation. It is good to be aware that there is a difference between having a demon and having a demonic manifestation. Having a demon means that an evil spirit is present and is at work in some way. This may happen in subtle, behind-the-scenes ways. But when a demon manifests, it makes itself known in a visible and more obvious way. Many times in the Gospel accounts, we see demons manifesting outwardly through a person. But it is significant to note that this is not the constant state of a demonized person. Let's look again at the example from Mark 1 that we looked at in Chapter One.

> *Then they went into Capernaum, and immediately on the Sabbath He entered the synagogue and taught. And they were astonished at His teaching, for He taught them as one having authority, and not as the scribes. Now there was a man in their synagogue with an unclean spirit. And he cried out, saying, "Let us alone! What have we to do with You, Jesus of Nazareth? Did You come to destroy us? I know who You are—the Holy One of God!" But Jesus rebuked him, saying, "Be quiet, and come out of him!" And when the unclean spirit had convulsed him and cried out with a loud voice, he came out of him* (Mark 1:21-26).

Here we have a scene where Jesus is teaching in a synagogue. The text says that there was a man in the synagogue "with an unclean spirit." In other words, he had a demon. It goes on to say that this unclean spirit began to speak through the person to Jesus; that is, it manifested. We don't know how long Jesus was teaching before the demon manifested, but it was long enough for the people to recognize that He taught with authority and not in the way they were used to the scribes teaching. This man was not in a constant state of having a demonic manifestation. Certainly, he would not have been allowed to come into the synagogue and listen to the teaching if he were. No, he was sitting there listening to Jesus teach with the rest of them. It is as though the authority that Jesus was teaching with forced the demon to show itself so that it could be cast out.

This type of scenario is sometimes referred to as a power encounter—where the Kingdom of God collides with the kingdom of darkness, forcing demons to manifest so that they can be driven out. This type of occurrence will usually happen during a time when the Holy Spirit is moving powerfully through preaching, worship, or prayer. It is worth noting that discernment is still required to recognize that it is in fact a demon that is manifesting in a situation like this. In other words, depending on the degree of manifestation it is possible for a demonic manifestation to go unnoticed or unrecognized, especially if there is no knowledge of deliverance ministry or where there is the belief that a Christian cannot have a demon.

When discerning outward demonic manifestations, I have learned to observe three specific areas: the person's countenance, body movements, and voice. A few years ago, I was praying for a woman at a healing service, and within seconds of prayer a demon began to manifest. I had simply welcomed the presence of the Holy Spirit, and she immediately began to shake. This can sometimes simply be a response to the Holy Spirit's power coming upon someone, but as I continued to pray the shaking became more violent and her countenance took on a tormented expression. I soon realized it was a demonic manifestation. As I commanded the power of the enemy to be broken, the woman screamed, fell to the ground, and received more prayer from those around her. Soon she was relieved as the demonic spirit left her.

I have noticed a pattern that whenever I preach and teach on the topic of deliverance from demons, some people who are under demonic influence will begin to experience manifestations while I am teaching. Sometimes this is visible—shaking, convulsing, a change in countenance, crying, or other outward signs. Many other times, it is something that they are experiencing internally but it is not observable outwardly. People have reported feeling something stirring in their stomach, feeling nauseous, sudden pain, irrational urges to leave the room, a feeling of being choked, or other inward symptoms of demons beginning to manifest. I have seen this happen so many times that I have come to expect it when I teach and minister on deliverance. I will tell people not to be afraid if this is happening, but that it is simply the evil spirits being agitated and getting nervous because they are about to be expelled.

I have also had people report that they have experienced demonic manifestations and received deliverance while reading my books and materials on deliverance or listening to one of my recorded sermons on the topic. If you have been experiencing some of the manifestations that I described in this section, don't be alarmed. Be encouraged that you are about to be set free. If you sense the need at any point as you read, turn to Appendix 3 at the end of this book and pray through the prayer for deliverance. Trust Jesus to set you free!

2. *Supernatural Discernment from the Holy Spirit*

Another way that demons can be discerned is through the gift of discerning of spirits. In First Corinthians 12, Paul lists nine supernatural gifts of the Holy Spirit that should be operating in the church and are available to believers. One of these gifts is called "discerning of spirits" (see 1 Corinthians 12:10). Discerning of spirits is particularly useful in the ministry of deliverance, although it is not limited to that purpose. It can be defined as the supernatural ability to perceive what is happening in the spiritual realm and judge between the Holy Spirit and demonic spirits.

The gift of discerning of spirits is not only for detecting evil spirits. It may function in recognizing the work of the Holy Spirit, like when John the Baptist "saw the Spirit descending from heaven like a dove, and He remained upon Him" (John 1:32). It also may work in being aware of the presence of angels, like when Elisha saw the army of angels surrounding him to protect him (see 2 Kings 6:14-17). For our purposes, we are considering how discerning of spirits operates to expose the presence of evil spirits.

The gift of discernment operates through our senses. Hebrews 5:14 puts it this way: "But solid food belongs to those who are of full age, that is, those who by reason of use have their senses exercised to discern both good and evil." Notice that it is "by reason of use" that discernment grows. The New American Standard Bible translates this phrase as "because of practice." In other words, part of how discerning spirits works is to experience something with one of our senses and then, over time and through more experience, begin to recognize what is happening in the spiritual realm. For example, some believers report seeing the presence of a demon as a creature, serpent, octopus, black spot, dark cloud, or other image. Others may feel something on their body or sense something in their spirit indicating a demonic presence. Sometimes it may come as an impression from the Holy Spirit about demonic activity or the specific name of a demon. Some people have reported smelling a distinct smell, such as sulfur or rotten eggs, indicating that an evil spirit is present.

While on staff at a church in Texas several years ago, I was praying for a woman at the altar one Sunday morning. She was a first-time visitor I had never met before. I prayed for her as I felt led by the Holy Spirit, but there was no indication that deliverance was needed. An intercessor who was standing behind her discerned that she had a spirit of fear, so I addressed this spirit. Immediately, the woman began to manifest a demon and receive deliverance. Not only was the spirit of fear cast out, but several other demons were expelled as well. It was the gift of discerning of spirits that exposed the presence of demons so that they could be addressed and cast out.

3. *Natural Discernment*

Another type of discernment is what I simply call natural discernment. The more experience you have with deliverance, the easier it becomes to discern the presence of evil spirits. I believe this is true of the supernatural discernment just mentioned, but also when it comes to observing natural signs and gaining information from the person to whom you are ministering. Understanding the various ways that demons can influence people can be very helpful when considering whether or not a person needs deliverance. It is also good to be aware of open doors and demonic entry points. For example, if you are ministering to a person and find out that they have been involved in the occult, there is a good chance that an evil spirit needs to be cast out. If there has been physical, sexual, or verbal abuse, it is common for demons to have entered in through that door. When signs of demonic influence are present—such as bondage, torment, oppression, or affliction—and open doors have occurred, you can deduce that deliverance is very likely needed.

Jesus did not rely solely on supernatural information when ministering deliverance. Sometimes, He simply asked questions to gain insight into the situation. This was the case when He set a boy free from an unclean spirit.

> *Then they brought him to Him. And when he saw Him, immediately the spirit convulsed him, and he fell on the ground and wallowed, foaming at the mouth. So He asked his father, "How long has this been happening to him?" And he said, "From childhood. And often he has thrown him*

both into the fire and into the water to destroy him" (Mark 9:20-22).

Notice first that this is another example of a demonic manifestation. The very presence of Jesus caused the demon to flare up, convulse the child, and throw him to the floor foaming at the mouth. But then also notice that Jesus asked a question to gain more information: "How long has this been happening to him?" It can often be very helpful to ask simple questions to help discern whether a demon is present and know how to minister effectively to the person in need. Several examples of questions could be given, but here are a few: How long have you been experiencing this problem? Are you aware of any open doors that allowed this spirit to be present? Did anything traumatic happen at the time this started? Are you aware of anyone against whom you are harboring unforgiveness? Are there any specific areas of sin that you think may have opened the door to this demon?

A young lady to whom my wife and I ministered was having recurring thoughts of death. For example, she would be driving down the road and suddenly imagine herself drifting off the road and crashing her car. She had overcome cancer a few years prior. Knowing her background and having learned that sometimes a spirit of death comes in during major and prolonged sicknesses, I suggested we pray for deliverance. Sure enough, as we prayed over her the Holy Spirit moved powerfully and she was delivered from the spirit of death, along with some other spirits.

A few years ago, I prayed for a young lady who had spent some time heavily involved in witchcraft before becoming a believer. She was struggling with torment, anxiety, and fear on a regular basis. It did not take the gift of discerning of spirits or a demonic manifestation to determine that there was a need for deliverance. The open doors in her life and the symptoms of demonic torment were enough to reveal the need to receive deliverance. Not surprisingly, as another woman and I prayed over her, demons began to manifest and be cast out.

I share these examples to show that discerning the presence of evil spirits can happen through knowing what to look for and being aware of the ways that demons operate. A time of deliverance does not always have to be initiated by a power encounter that causes a demonic manifestation or the gift of discerning of spirits exposing a demon. When doors have been opened up to evil spirits, and when some of the common signs of demonic influence are present, there is a good chance that a demon is at work and deliverance is needed. Keep in mind though that every case is unique and it is always necessary to seek the guidance of the Holy Spirit for each situation.

Key 2: Discovering and Closing Any Open Doors

In Chapter Two, I mentioned that one of the truths about demonic influence is that there are certain things that can open the door to evil spirits. Demons cannot simply go into any person they please; there is normally a point of access that they enter through. An important part of the deliverance process is to close these doors. This will not only greatly aid the process of deliverance; it will also help with long-term freedom and wholeness.

If we want deliverance, we must be willing to break every agreement with the devil and completely align ourselves with God. Closing the doors means that we are taking away every right that the enemy has gained to our lives and shutting every point of access. We position ourselves to resist the devil when we are first submitted to God (see James 4:7).

- If a door has been opened through embracing sin, you must come into the light, confess your sin freely, and repent of it totally. There can be no justifying of sin, and you must truly want to be free from it.

63

- If you have had any involvement in the occult, there must be a complete renunciation and a willingness to rid yourself of anything related to occult or New Age influence.

- If you are harboring bitterness, anger, or unforgiveness toward anybody, you must be willing to forgive those people from your heart.

- If generational curses or strongholds are present in your family line, shutting this door could look like looking to the cross and renouncing the sins of previous generations.

- If ungodly soul ties have been created through sexual sin or abusive relationships, cut those ties and sever yourself from that relationship.

When closing doors and praying through prayers of deliverance, sincerity in these matters is critical. Deliverance should not be seen as a rote formula to robotically pray through but a sincere expression of desperation for Jesus to set you free. Both God and the devil know when we are genuine and serious about freedom. Ask the Lord to do the work in your heart and prepare the ground so that there is no hindrance to receiving the freedom that you desire.

Another point about closing doors is that it is often helpful to be as specific as possible. When I lead deliverance prayers for closing doors, I will often start in a general way but then allow space for people to pray very specifically. Confess sin in general, but then also confess and repent of specific sins that have opened the door. It is not uncommon for a premeditated sinful choice such as adultery, stealing, or abortion to open a door to unclean spirits. Name things like this that are relevant and agree with God about them. When closing the door of unforgiveness, name the specific people whom you are forgiving and release them to God. Renounce any occult activities that you have engaged in, calling them out by name. The point here is to be clear, thorough, and specific when closing the door on the devil.

There have been times in a ministry session when we came to an apparent standstill. Demons were manifesting, but were not seeming to leave when commands were made. At times like this it might be tempting to shout louder and try harder, but I have found that a better approach is to take time to ask the Holy Spirit for direction and revelation about what is going on. In situations like this, there can sometimes be a specific door that needs to be closed. God may reveal it to someone who is ministering or may show the one who is receiving ministry. Once that door is closed, resume the process of driving out the demons.

Throughout this book, there will be several prayers to close specific doors of demonic access. You can pray through various areas like this one by one, focusing on a specific facet at a time. And Appendix 3 contains a thorough prayer that you can use to walk through closing multiple doors in one sitting. I have used prayers like this on many occasions and can attest to their effectiveness when prayed with sincerity and a true desire for freedom. If you believe you need deliverance, I encourage you to pray through the prayers in this book with expectation for God to meet you and bring greater freedom to your life.

Key 3: Driving Out Evil Spirits

Once you have closed all known doors, it is time to drive out any evil spirits that are present. When it comes to casting out demons, we see an example to follow from the apostle Paul: "But Paul...turned and said to the spirit, 'I command you in the name of Jesus Christ to come out of her'" (Acts 16:18). Paul spoke directly to the demon, and he did it in the name of Jesus. This is how we are to deal with evil spirits when receiving deliverance or when ministering it to others. We are to make forceful words of command, exercising the authority that we have been given in the name of Jesus. There may be times when intercession is helpful in aiding the process of deliverance. But generally speaking, when it comes to casting out demons we are not so much praying to God but speaking directly to demons, commanding them to come out. This is the way that Jesus ministered and the way that the early church followed.

This is where it is important to remember that as believers in Christ, we have authority over every demon. We do not need to be afraid of them; we should have absolute confidence in our position in Christ. Jesus said this: "Behold, I give you the authority to trample on serpents and scorpions, and over all the power of the enemy, and nothing shall by any means hurt you. Nevertheless do not rejoice in this, that the spirits are subject to you, but rather rejoice because your names are written in heaven" (Luke 10:19-20). Our ultimate joy does not come from our authority over demons. But never forget, evil spirits are subject to us in the name of Jesus. Mark 16:17 says, "And these signs will follow those who believe: In My name they will cast out demons."

It is often helpful and beneficial to have one or two solid believers to stand with you and pray over you for deliverance. But many people who are in need of freedom do not know where to turn and don't have anybody who believes in deliverance to pray in faith with them. As you stand on the Word and have confidence in your authority over evil spirits, it is possible to pray and drive out evil spirits from yourself without anyone else being present. There are many testimonies of this happening, and it is sometimes referred to as *self-deliverance*. If you are in severe bondage or torment and do not have the faith to pray over yourself, it would be ideal to have someone else pray over you who has experience in this area and has a heart of compassion for those needing deliverance. Follow God's leading and know that He desires you to be free from demonic influence and all captivity.

When evil spirits leave a person, it may happen in a variety of ways. There will often be a tangible sign of the spirit leaving, but this is not always the case. I have found—and this is confirmed by others—that the most common way for a demon to leave is through the mouth. This often happens with coughing, deep sighing, burping, yawning, screaming, and sometimes even vomiting. Other times people have reported feeling spirits exiting through their hands or feet, lifting off of their head, or other observable ways. People often say that they feel lighter once demons have been expelled. And sometimes there are no observable manifestations or release, but the fruit of deliverance is evident after the prayer time.

In driving out demons, it is important to stand in a position of authority and not be intimidated. Don't be alarmed, frightened, or caught off guard by any manifestations that might occur. If a demon is being stubborn and resisting being expelled, continue to make commands until it exits, or seek more specific guidance from the Holy Spirit about what is happening and how to proceed. Jesus is your Deliverer and all authority is in His name!

| 5 |

FORGIVENESS OPENS
THE PRISON DOOR

Janice had been through severe abuse in her childhood. When another woman and I met to pray for her, she opened up about the sexual abuse and coverups that had happened in her family. She shared how some family members, who were seen in the public eye as godly church members, were actually sexually molesting and raping young women, including her. She shared how she had been impregnated through this as a teenager, and how her mother had forced her to get an abortion in order to conceal what had happened. After experiencing all of this trauma, God had broken through in His grace and she was on a path of restoration many years later.

As I led her through a prayer for deliverance, she came to the point of forgiving the ones who had abused her. Tears flowed from her eyes and the atmosphere was filled with the love of God. I began to weep as she verbalized her forgiveness of those who had done her unthinkable damage. As she forgave, a prison door was opened for her to step out into greater freedom and healing, and powerful deliverance took place.

Opening the Prison Door

Like Janice's testimony, I have noticed that quite often the most powerful time during personal deliverance sessions or corporate prayers for deliverance is the part when people pray to forgive those who have sinned against them. The love of God comes in a tangible way, tears run down faces, and spiritual chains begin to melt. Hearts begin to heal from years of pain, disappointment, and abuse. Powers of darkness lose their hold as forgiveness is received from God and extended to others. Light comes in, the prison door is opened, and captives are set free.

We live in a broken world that is full of broken people. It is inevitable that as we walk through life, we will experience hurt and be sinned against by others to one degree or another. How we respond to these situations has a dramatic impact on our destiny. If we harbor hatred, resentment, and unforgiveness, we will end up in a spiritual prison. The longer we stay in this prison of unforgiveness, the more torment and affliction we welcome into our lives. But through the key of forgiveness, the prison door is opened.

Part of the commission of Jesus was to open prison doors: "To proclaim liberty to the captives, and the opening of the prison to those who are bound" (Isaiah 61:1). I believe that forgiveness is a major way that the prison door is opened so that captives can be set free. As unforgiveness places us in a spiritual prison, extending forgiveness swings the prison door wide open.

In this chapter, we will look at the powerful nature of forgiveness. We will also overcome some common misconceptions about forgiveness that have sometimes added more pain to people instead of bringing healing. Forgiveness is easy to talk about, but harder to apply in practical experience. But we must embrace forgiveness, as it is a key aspect of being a follower of Jesus and critical to setting captives free.

A Parable About Forgiveness

There are various teachings on forgiveness throughout the New Testament. It is a significant theme that is worthy of our time and attention. One of the largest passages that deals with the topic is a parable that Jesus told in Matthew 18. Take time to read through this story, slowly taking in what is being communicated.

> *Then Peter came to Him and said, "Lord, how often shall my brother sin against me, and I forgive him? Up to seven times?" Jesus said to him, "I do not say to you, up to seven times, but up to seventy times seven. Therefore the kingdom of heaven is like a certain king who wanted to settle accounts with his servants. And when he had begun to settle accounts, one was brought to him who owed him ten thousand talents. But as he was not able to pay, his master commanded that he be sold, with his wife and children and all that he had, and that payment be made. The servant therefore fell down before him, saying, 'Master, have patience with me, and I will pay you all.' Then the master of that servant was moved with compassion, released him, and forgave him the debt. But that servant went out and found one of his fellow servants who owed him a hundred denarii; and he laid hands on him and took him by the throat, saying, 'Pay me what you owe!' So his fellow servant fell down at his feet and begged him, saying, 'Have patience with me, and I will pay you all.' And he would not, but went and threw him into prison till he should pay the debt. So when his fellow servants saw what had been*

*done, they were very grieved, and came and told their master
all that had been done. Then his master, after he had called
him, said to him, 'You wicked servant! I forgave you all that
debt because you begged me. Should you not also have had
compassion on your fellow servant, just as I had pity on you?'
And his master was angry, and delivered him to the torturers
until he should pay all that was due to him. So My heavenly
Father also will do to you if each of you, from his heart, does
not forgive his brother his trespasses"* (Matthew 18:21-35).

Forgiveness has Two Sides

Peter asked Jesus a question about how many times he should extend forgiveness to someone who sins against him. I imagine that he thought Jesus would be pretty impressed with his offer to forgive up to seven times. But Jesus raised the bar. His use of "seventy times seven" was a way of essentially saying: *Lose track of how many times you forgive. You should always forgive those who sin against you.* He went on to explain Himself with a parable about servants and a king.

One of the things that we learn from this parable is that forgiveness has two sides. I like to say that forgiveness is like a coin; it has two sides and you can't take one side without the other. One side of the coin is that we receive forgiveness from God. The other side of the coin is that we extend forgiveness to others. Consider this well-known statement from the Lord's prayer: "And forgive us our debts, as we also have forgiven our debtors" (Matthew 6:12 ESV). Here again, we see the two sides of forgiveness paired together.

The servant in the parable was delighted to have his debt erased, but was not willing to extend the same benefit to his fellow servant who owed him a much smaller amount. He wanted one side of forgiveness but not the other. The end result was that he ended up in a prison, tormented by torturers. I believe this is a clear symbolic picture of what happens in the spiritual realm when we walk in unforgiveness, bitterness, and resentment. It gives demonic spirits access to torment and oppress us, and it places us in captivity.

Let's take a closer look at these two sides of forgiveness.

1. Receiving Forgiveness from God

The servant in the parable owed the king a debt that he could never pay back. Jesus' use of ten thousand talents is meant to portray such a large amount that the servant would not be able to get out of debt, even though he pleaded with the king for patience and promised to pay back what he owed. Faced with the prospect of being sold into slavery along with his wife and children, he begged for mercy. The king was moved with compassion and released the servant from the whole debt. Can you imagine the weight that was lifted off of his shoulders? Can you imagine the joy that flooded his soul?

Those of us who have experienced the forgiveness of God should be able to relate to this. We too had a debt that we could never pay. We too faced dire consequences for our sinful actions. We too came to God in repentance and asked for mercy. And we too have had the debt of sin lifted off of our shoulders. We must never forget this beautiful experience of God's love and forgiveness, freely given to us because Jesus has paid our debt!

It is in light of the mercy and forgiveness of God that He calls us to forgive others. We receive forgiveness from Him and we extend forgiveness to others.

2. Extending Forgiveness to Others

When the man who had received such an extravagant gift of forgiveness came across a fellow servant, he remembered that this man owed him some money. The amount of 100 denarii that Jesus used is intentionally exponentially smaller than the amount that the servant had just been forgiven of. While it was a valid debt, it was not even close to comparable. This demonstrates that while the sin of others against us is real, it is actually miniscule in comparison to what our sin against God equates to. To be clear, this does not justify the sin against us or make it any less painful. It simply puts things in a different perspective. What made the king so upset in the story is that the servant refused to extend the same forgiveness to others that he had just received. It is in view of the work of the cross and the price that Jesus paid for us to be forgiven that God commands us to forgive others.

We must learn to walk in forgiveness toward the ones who have sinned against us or caused us pain. This can be difficult to do, especially when the hurt is deep and the pain is real. But God will give us the grace to forgive from the heart. He will help us and enable us to release the ones who have hurt us, intentionally or unintentionally.

Harboring bitterness, resentment, or unforgiveness toward others is a major open door for evil spirits. It is important to understand that withholding forgiveness from others does not hurt them; it hurts you. Unforgiveness puts us into a spiritual prison and gives the devil God-given permission to torment us—not because God wants us to be tormented but because we have violated the principles of His Word. Unforgiveness that continues to go unchecked is a serious issue and a major root cause for many other problems.

If you are struggling to forgive, remember that forgiveness is first a choice, not a feeling. Don't wait until you feel like forgiving. Your heart will catch up as you exercise your will and release the ones who have sinned against you. God will give you the grace to forgive as you step out and obey Him. You can spend time in prayer and verbalize your forgiveness between you and the Lord. When you do this, you are taking a major step to allowing God to heal your heart and are freeing yourself from demonic captivity. Look to Jesus, the One who while dying on the cross said, "Father, forgive them, for they do not know what they do" (Luke 23:34). Walking in forgiveness can be a process, so take whatever steps you can take at this time. You may need to continually release the people to God as you walk the forgiveness out.

What Forgiveness Does *Not* Mean

Sometimes, teaching on forgiveness has been misunderstood and misapplied, causing even more damage to a person who has already been severely wounded or abused. And sometimes a person's reluctance to forgive is based on a misunderstanding of what it means and does *not* mean to forgive. Therefore, it is important to make the following clarifications:

1. Forgiveness does not minimize the damage done.

It is important to reiterate that forgiving someone does not mean that what they did was okay or that the hurt you experienced is not real. Forgiveness does not minimize or justify abusive, deceptive, or hypocritical behavior. It is not a call to just stuff everything down, pretend like nothing ever happened, or sweep everything under the rug. It is simply saying that you are releasing that person to God and forgiving them because God has forgiven you.

Rather than stuffing the trauma and pain of what happened, it is good to process the pain in a healthy way. It often helps to do this with the help of trusted friends, mentors, pastors, or counselors, depending on the severity and nature of what you have experienced. But you can process the pain, take it to God, heal, and move forward in a productive way.

2. Forgiveness does not mean reconciliation.

Extending forgiveness does not mean that you necessarily need to communicate anything to the person who hurt you. This will often depend on the specifics of the circumstances. But know that you can process pain with the Lord, allow the Holy Spirit to move in your heart, and pray prayers of forgiveness without involving the person you are forgiving. You can let go of any resentment, hatred, or bitterness that is in your heart. Although forgiveness is related to damage done by another person, it is primarily a transaction between you and God. In fact, sometimes the ones you need to forgive have since passed away.

Forgiveness does not mean that you must automatically reconcile with the person who hurt you. It takes one person to forgive, but it takes two willing people to reconcile. While reconciliation is ideal, it is not always possible when a person persists in unrepentant sin and ungodly actions. You do not need to continually put yourself in situations where you are being abused. Reconciliation can happen if the person shows the fruit of genuine repentance, but that is out of your control.

Let me give a few illustrations to explain this point. Let's suppose that you hire a person to do work on your house, and they rip you off and don't fulfill their obligation. You can forgive that person, but you can also choose to never hire them again for house repairs. To use a more serious situation, suppose that it comes to light that a babysitter sexually abused one of your children while you were away from the house. You can forgive the babysitter, but you may never want to allow them into your home again, and certainly not alone with your children.

The point I am making is that you can extend forgiveness and maintain boundaries at the same time. Some have been pressured to "forgive and forget" in such a way that has caused them to be re-abused continually. This is not healthy and is a misapplication of forgiveness. Yes, we must always forgive. But we can allow time for trust to be rebuilt and look for repentance before taking steps toward reconciliation. Forgiveness is always something you can do regardless of the other person's actions. Reconciliation is a separate thing and requires active participation of the other party involved.

A Prayer to Extend Forgiveness

The following prayer is a model for how you can pray to extend forgiveness to those who have sinned against you or hurt you in any way. Take time to meditate on what Jesus has done for you. Reflect on God's forgiveness of you and the price that was paid. Receive a fresh revelation of what the blood of Jesus has accomplished for you and allow God's love to fill your heart. Take steps to forgive, and ask God to help you where you are struggling to let go of resentment or bitterness.

If you sense that unforgiveness is lingering, continue to pray through this prayer over the course of several days or weeks. Allow the Holy Spirit to do a deep work in you so that more healing and freedom can come. Find a quiet place where you can spend quality time with God and use the following words to guide you, adding your own words where appropriate.

Heavenly Father, I thank You for the gift of salvation and forgiveness through Your Son, Jesus. I ask for a fresh revelation of what it means to be forgiven and have the burden of sin removed from my shoulders. Help me to forgive completely and thoroughly and to let go of any bitterness or resentment. Give me the grace to forgive, and lead me into more healing by the Holy Spirit.

Because You have forgiven me, I choose to freely forgive anyone who has ever sinned against me or hurt me in any way. I release them to You and let go of all bitterness, anger, hatred, and resentment. Specifically, I forgive _____.

I let these people go and release them to You, Father. I choose to bless them and place them in Your hands. Pour the Holy Spirit into my heart and bring healing to areas that are broken. Right now, I step out of the prison of unforgiveness. And in the name of Jesus, I command any unclean spirits that are in my life because of unforgiveness to come out. Go, in the name of Jesus!

BREAKING THE CHAINS OF BONDAGE

O ver the last five chapters, we have covered foundational truths about demons and deliverance. I wanted to lay a foundation that will help you understand how to recognize how evil spirits gain access to people's lives and how to get free from their grip. We will now look to cover some specific types of demonic influence. In this chapter, we will deal with breaking the chains of *bondage*.

Removing the Graveclothes

When explaining the nature of deliverance ministry, I often teach on the story of Jesus raising Lazarus from the dead. While it is a powerful miracle and a demonstration of Christ Himself being the resurrection and the life, this story also carries symbolism that shows the need for deliverance from demonic influence. Below is the account of when Jesus came to the tomb to raise Lazarus up.

> *Now when He had said these things, He cried with a loud voice, "Lazarus, come forth!" And he who had died came out bound hand and foot with graveclothes, and his face was wrapped with a cloth. Jesus said to them, "Loose him, and let him go"* (John 11:43-44).

Notice that when Jesus raised Lazarus from the dead, He gave two commands. The first was, "Lazarus, come forth!" Lazarus emerged from the tomb perfectly alive, but he was still bound with grave-clothes. So the next command was "Loose him, and let him go."

Many Christians today find themselves like Lazarus was in between these two commands. They are alive from the dead spiritually through salvation in Christ, but they are wrapped in spiritual graveclothes of bondage and oppression. Like Lazarus, their feet are bound up, keeping them from being able to run the race set before them. Their hands are tied, keeping them from serving as they are intended. Their faces are wrapped, keeping them from knowing their true identity in Christ. They have received God's forgiveness and are alive spiritually, but they are still bound in certain areas of their lives.

These believers know what it means to be forgiven, but they are not experiencing the full freedom that Christ purchased for them on the cross. They have heard the message of salvation ("Lazarus, come forth!") but not the message of deliverance ("Loose him, and let him go"). They sometimes find themselves in a cycle of defeat—bound by fear, addiction, depression, wounds of the past, bitterness, sin, or other bondages. It's hard to function when you're wrapped in graveclothes. But I have seen time and again how people begin to grow rapidly after being set free from the influence of evil spirits.

God never intended salvation without deliverance. He not only wants us to be forgiven, but also free. While deliverance ministry is certainly not a cure-all, and not all problems are caused by demons, there are many sincere believers who are bound by demonic chains and need the ministry of deliverance.

The Devil Is a Tempter

In dealing with bondage, we are specifically referring to how evil spirits can be involved in keeping people enslaved to sinful habits or destructive addictions. The devil works overtime to lure people and draw them into sin. He even tried to entice the Son of God when He came. Notice that the following passage refers to him as "the tempter."

> *Then Jesus was led up by the Spirit into the wilderness to be tempted by the devil. And when He had fasted forty days and forty nights, afterward He was hungry. Now when the tempter came to Him, he said, "If You are the Son of God, command that these stones become bread"* (Matthew 4:1-3).

One of the characteristics of satan is that he is a tempter. We see from the first time he appears in Scripture as the serpent in the Garden of Eden that the devil is a master at temptation, using deceptive methods and appealing to mankind's innate desires. He twists truth and plants seeds to try to pull people into all kinds of sin and disobedience to God. He makes sin look appealing, highlighting its pleasures while cloaking its destructive nature.

It would make logical sense that demons, like the devil whom they serve, would also be masters at temptation. While we all face temptation simply by living in a fallen world, and while much temptation is simply a work of the flesh, we also need to be aware that sometimes the temptations that come to us have a demonic origin. A lying spirit seeks to compel you to tell lies (or to believe the enemy's lies). A spirit of adultery tries to push you toward being unfaithful to your spouse. A spirit of anger compels you to uncontrollable rage. These are very real spiritual realities, and many other examples could be given.

We need not be alarmed or frazzled when we face temptations; it is part of life on earth, and Jesus faced temptations of every kind. Instead of being caught off guard, we can follow the example of Jesus to defeat every temptation by using the Word of God as our weapon. We must be vigilant and on guard, ready to stand against the devil, deny the flesh, and walk in the power of the Spirit.

When Sin Turns into Bondage

While the devil is a tempter, his goal is not simply to lure us with sin, but to enslave us to it. He knows that sin left unchecked has a way of becoming stronger and stronger until it begins to master us. Jesus affirmed this when He said, "Truly, truly, I say to you, everyone who practices sin is a slave to sin" (John 8:34 ESV). A person who has become enslaved to sin is in *bondage*.

At this point, I want to make it clear that there is a difference between a person who is in rebellion and a person who is in bondage. A person living in rebellion is in outright disobedience to God, knows it, and likes it. They have no genuine sorrow for sin, no real desire to be free from it, and willfully run from God. They might feel condemned or ashamed if they get caught by others, but this is not the same as repentance. The person who is in bondage, on the other hand, is seeking to live a holy life but cannot seem to get free in certain areas. It could be lustful thoughts, a drawing toward pornography, addiction to a substance, constant temptation to lie, anger issues, or various other enslavements. This is a person who genuinely wants to be free, but cannot seem to break the chains that bind him, no matter what he tries.

The Bible is clear that Christians should not be living in bondage to sin: "For sin shall not have dominion over you, for you are not under law but under grace" (Romans 6:14). While we won't walk in perfection, freedom should be the norm, not enslavement. When a person sincerely desires to be free and has a repentant heart, yet still cannot seem to overcome a sinful practice, it is possible that what they are dealing with is not simply the flesh that needs to be crucified, but a demon that needs to be cast out. When there is an enslavement to sin or a harmful practice, deliverance needs to be considered as a possible solution. I have seen people set free from various types of bondage to sinful and destructive practices through deliverance from demons.

Let's take anger as an example. The book of Ephesians gives us this admonition: "'Be angry, and do not sin': do not let the sun go down on your wrath, nor give place to the devil" (Ephesians 4:26-27). Anger is a human emotion, and as such it is not sinful in itself to experience anger. God Himself expresses anger at times, and when Jesus walked the earth, there were times when He demonstrated righteous anger. But "fits of anger" is also named among the sinful works of the flesh (see Galatians 5:20 ESV). Anger that is not properly handled will turn into sin. And if this sin is not dealt with, it will eventually give "place to the devil" and lead to demonic bondage.

When anger becomes uncontrollable and compulsive, there could be a demonic spirit of anger involved. You will hear people say things like, "Something just came over me" or "I don't know what happened, I just kind of snapped." Others will notice the shift when the person loses control and is being influenced by another force. Many people have found that they could control their temper once they were delivered from a spirit of anger.

The same progression that Paul outlined regarding anger in Ephesians 4 can be applied to just about any type of sinful activity. When sin goes unchecked and undealt with, a door can be opened up for an unclean spirit to create a bondage to that sin. This is one of the reasons why it is important to walk in the light and keep short accounts with God through confession and repentance.

Unclean Spirits and Sexual Sin

Sexual sin is an area that many people find themselves enslaved to. Because sex is a natural human appetite that involves pleasure, it has been a major target of the enemy throughout history. And because sexual intimacy is so closely linked to the sacred covenant of marriage and is the means of procreation, satan has a particular interest in distorting and defiling human sexuality.

To be clear, God is not anti-sex. He designed sexual intimacy to be a unique bond between a husband and wife in the context of the covenant of marriage. But He is very much against sexual immorality. Any type of sexual activity outside of His established parameters is a perversion of His design. Sexual intimacy before marriage, adultery, homosexuality, pornography, lust, unclean fantasy, and many other examples of sexual immorality could be given.

God is not trying to keep us from having a good time by confining sex to the marriage covenant. He is the Creator. He knows how we are meant to function and His ways are best. He knows that while sexual sin might bring momentary pleasure, it always comes at the price of causing long-term damage to ourselves and others. When we engage in sexual sin, we are not only sinning against God, we are also sinning against our own body: "Flee sexual immorality. Every sin that a man does is outside the body, but he who commits sexual immorality sins against his own body" (1 Corinthians 6:18).

The topic of sexual sin must absolutely be addressed by the Church in this hour. It is prominently named among sins throughout the entire New Testament. We've sometimes been guilty of pointing the finger at the world for its sexual perversion while immorality runs rampant in our own house. While we should stand against the tide of immorality in our society, we don't have any business judging the world for sexual sin; that is what they know. But there must be a difference in the people of God.

> *For this is the will of God, your sanctification: that you should abstain from sexual immorality; that each of you should know how to possess his own vessel in sanctification and honor, not in passion of lust, like the Gentiles who do not know God...For God did not call us to uncleanness, but in holiness* (1 Thessalonians 4:3-5,7).

Because sexual sin has become so common in our culture, it can be easy to become desensitized to it and minimize the severity of it. But make no mistake—sexual sin has serious consequences and should never be seen as normal for believers. By the grace of God and power of the Holy Spirit, we should be able to walk in holiness and freedom. If a person is genuinely seeking to walk in sexual purity but can't break free, they have become enslaved and might need deliverance from demonic chains of bondage.

One of the terms for *demons* in the Bible is *unclean spirits*. I have come to see that unclean spirits can be involved in keeping people in bondage to all types of sexual immorality. Like anger, sexual sin can be a work of the flesh. But when it becomes compulsive and enslaving, we should consider that there might be a demonic influence that needs to be expelled. The following testimony of deliverance from pornography illustrates this truth.

Set Free from Pornography

Pornography has become a major pandemic in our world, and this stronghold is wreaking havoc in lives, families, and the Church as a whole. For some people, the key for getting free from the grip of pornography will be deliverance from unclean spirits. Such was the case for Jason.

Jason had been married for ten years at the time I prayed for him. Throughout the entirety of his marriage he had struggled with addiction to pornography, and as would be expected, this put a strain on the relationship. He would have short periods of victory but could never seem to attain lasting freedom.

Looking for help and permanent change, Jason attended a men's retreat with the topic of walking in sexual purity. I was one of the speakers and my message was on repentance and deliverance. I shared how sexual sin can often be influenced by unclean spirits, especially when the behavior is compulsive and enslaving. Jesus came to set us free from the power of sin and the kingdom of darkness. For someone to be set free from sexual sin—or any sin for that matter—requires genuine repentance. But if there is a demonic element to the bondage to sin, casting out evil spirits is also an important aspect of finding true freedom.

After I finished the message, I led the whole group of men in a prayer of repentance. Then I began to take authority over unclean spirits and command them to leave in the name of Jesus. When I prayed for Jason, I laid hands on him and commanded the spirits of lust and pornography to come out of him. (I didn't know anything about his situation at the time; I simply prayed as I felt led by the Holy Spirit.) He immediately doubled over as if he had been punched in the gut, and he felt as though something came out of him.

A year later, Jason attended the same retreat. Except this time, he was not there to receive ministry but to help minister to others. He testified that he had not viewed pornography since the prayer for deliverance a year prior. For the first time in over ten years, he was truly free!

Jason's freedom did not come until he was set free from the influence of unclean spirits. Once the demons were gone, the nature of his battle changed dramatically. It is not that he never experienced temptation again; but now he was free to deny lust and choose purity. There was no longer an internal compulsion that seemed out of his control. The cycle of defeat was over and the chains of bondage had been broken.

Not Just a Men's Problem

Pornography and various other types of sexual sin are certainly not just a men's problem. Women can struggle with lust, seduction, fornication, and other types of immorality. There is often a hidden shame that goes along with this and women can feel trapped and isolated, believing that there is no one to talk to or receive help from.

Church should be a place where people are safe to confess sins in order to find freedom: "Therefore, confess your sins to one another and pray for one another, that you may be healed" (James 5:16 ESV). There is power in walking in the light, and shame is lifted off when we confess sins and receive forgiveness and cleansing. This obviously applies to both men and women. But it can be particularly hard for women struggling with sexual issues to share about their bondage in this area. Wisdom and care should be exercised about whom things are shared with, but women will find breakthrough and deliverance when they bring their struggle to the light with safe people.

A particular testimony comes to mind along these lines. Olivia was a young woman receiving prayer at the front of the church. I had preached a message on deliverance and people were receiving ministry. The lady who was praying for Olivia called me over to help. When I came to minister to her, I asked what area she needed freedom in. Without hesitation, she freely admitted that she struggled with masturbation, and that it was a source of comfort, especially when she was anxious. As I led her to repent and renounce the unclean spirit behind this, she let out a loud shriek, dropped to her knees, and was instantly delivered.

For men and women alike, when it comes to issues of bondage to sexual sin, we must consider the role that deliverance has in setting captives free.

Delivered from an Eating Disorder

Food addictions and eating disorders are another area where deliverance can be a key factor. Like sex, food is a natural appetite that can become perverted when it becomes an idol in our lives. The following testimony is from my sister, who has been free from an eating disorder for almost fifteen years now:

> I would say that the bondage that I experienced with an eating disorder probably started in my middle school years. It started out simply by having an unhealthy relationship with food. Food became way too important to me and I began to basically center my life around it. This progressed into my high school years and it gradually became worse.
>
> I'm not sure exactly when the demonic influence entered the scene but I would say it was probably my junior or senior year of high school. My eating at this point began spiraling out of control. I would physically feel something come over me. I could feel it all over my face and it truly felt like I had no control over my eating. I would binge eat and then feel so much shame and regret for doing it (especially since there is so much pressure for women in our society to look a certain way). I would feel so depressed every time I would binge eat but also feel so

helpless about it because every time that darkness came over me it felt like a switch was flipped and I would lose control over what I was doing. Feeling like I had no control led me to seek out a way to get rid of (or "purge") the food I had just eaten. After I would binge, I would work out for hours hoping to burn up the calories I had just eaten. Then I discovered an easier way to "purge." I would use coffee (made super strong/dark) to make the food go right through me. I never really thought I had a disorder or was bulimic because I wasn't physically making myself throw up. That was how I justified it in my mind.

At this point in my life I was so depressed and miserable. I truly thought to myself that this was just a part of who I was and that it was something I was going to have to battle for the rest of my life. I didn't see a way out and this was extremely depressing. During my freshman to sophomore year in college I really began to read the Bible and search the Scriptures. I read so many verses about how we are to walk in freedom and couldn't understand why I wasn't. After all, I was a Christian. So why wasn't I experiencing the freedom and joy in Christ that I was supposed to be experiencing? I can remember praying, "God, if this is how it's going to be for the rest of my life then I don't want to be here."

I am so thankful that God showed me that it didn't have to be that way and that He led me on a path of deliverance. The first step in this journey was for me to realize that my unhealthy obsession with food was a sin. I was putting food and my self-image before God. I was, in a sense, worshiping those things instead of God. It was the first time I had thought of it in that way. I repented of this and asked God for forgiveness. God then began to reveal to me that the battle I was facing was not against "flesh and blood." It was against demonic forces. The bondage I was facing was demonic in nature. I had a prayer time with my brother, Jake, and this was the beginning of the deliverance process.

The more I learned about deliverance and about spiritual battles, the more I was convinced that I was under demonic oppression. I began to fight my battle differently once I came to this realization—praying against the demonic forces, commanding evil spirits to go, using Scripture to fight against the powers of darkness. My deliverance didn't come right away and I would say it was due to the fact that I was afraid to give Jesus complete control over it. I thought, if Jesus is the One who sets me free, then would He at some point take His hand off of my life and allow me to go back into bondage? I thought if I was "in control" of my deliverance (even though this is impossible) I could make sure that I would not go back. This showed my lack of understanding of the nature and character of God. He loves us and wants to see us set free, but it has to be on His terms and in His way—not ours. If we could set ourselves free then we could claim some "glory" in it. But all glory must go to Jesus. It is only by His blood and His working that we can be free. We don't get to take any credit for it.

It was when I came to this realization—that it was all His working and that He was faithful, that He would deliver me and continue to keep me free, that I didn't have to be afraid of going back into bondage—it was when I realized these things that my freedom truly came. I remember it was on Saint Patrick's Day of 2006. That night I cried out to God in my bedroom and asked Him to take this bondage from me. I surrendered to Him and truly believed that it was only by His power that I could be set free. I fell asleep and woke up some time later and felt that I had to throw up. I went to the bathroom and threw up several times. This was not the result of a physical illness; it was a manifestation of deliverance, and spirits were leaving me. For the first time in a long time I felt a peace. I felt like something was different. I felt that I had been set free.

From that point on things were completely different. I no longer felt like I was a slave to food or that it controlled me. I will say, I did have to relearn how to have a healthy relationship with food. I had been that way for so long that I had to train myself to know the right portion sizes and to stop eating when I was full. But I no longer felt out of control. I was able to stop eating when I was full and was able to control myself.

That person, who was under so much bondage, truly feels like it wasn't even me when I look back and think about that time in my life. It's like the Scripture says— we are a new creation. I don't even recognize the old me. Jesus has made me into someone completely different, and I am eternally grateful for the freeing power of His blood. He paid such a dear price so that we could walk in freedom on this earth!

There is so much we can learn from this testimony. It demonstrates the deceptive nature of sin and how it can turn into bondage over time. It shows the need for repentance, but also for deliverance from demonic powers. It also teaches the need for the renewing of the mind once deliverance has happened. Praise God for a life set free and transformed!

Breaking the Chains of Addiction

What about addictions to substances? Can there be a demonic influence in alcoholism, drug abuse, and other addictions? Yes, absolutely. Drug use and demonic influence go hand in hand, and using illicit drugs can be a gateway to evil spirits. We are told to be sober-minded and self-controlled. Drunkenness is a sin that leads to debauchery (see Ephesians 5:18). Altering our state of mind can open us up to demonic spirits, not to mention the bondage and enslavement to the drugs or alcohol that can happen.

Below is a testimony from a friend of mine who is involved in leadership at Threshold Church, where I serve as pastor. He and his wife went to pray for a friend of theirs who had a long-standing addiction to heroin. At the time they prayed for him, they were newer to our church and deliverance was a relatively new concept for them.

> My wife and I had been attending Threshold Church for a little over a year prior to this deliverance experience. Prior to attending Threshold under the ministry of Pastor Jake, we had a very basic understanding of deliverance. We understood the importance and need for Christians to be set free, but up to this point we had never experienced an actual deliverance. So the testimony we are about to share is one that comes from a place of humility and brokenness for those who need to be set free.
>
> In 2016 we planned a trip to Florida to visit some close friends. We had made the decision to take the whole family, which included our two small children, both under

two years of age at the time. The purpose of this visit was not to see the beautiful ocean or to enjoy a relaxing vacation. The purpose for this trip was to see our dear friend, who had been addicted to heroin for over 10 years, set free. We purposely didn't tell close family and friends about our trip because we didn't want the words of fear and doubt to consume our thoughts and speech.

We made the choice to stay in our friend's home during this trip with the intention of having the opportunity to comfort his wife and possibly pray with them as a couple. Our friend was actively using during our stay so it was difficult to have logical conversations. However, this wasn't going to stop us; we had been sent on a mission and we desired to see it completed.

It was our last night in Florida and we had yet to see any signs of our friend wanting to be set free, but the Spirit of our God had plans for that night, plans that would change all of our lives. Around 9:00 PM we asked our friend again if he was ready to be free. He stated, "No, not yet." This was hard to hear but we kept pressing him and asking. Finally, around 9:30 PM he walked out of his bedroom with his small bag of heroin and needles. He then said, "I'm ready." At first this came as a shock, but we quickly moved to action. We took him outside and burned the remaining bag of heroin in a bonfire. During this time, he kept stating, "I can't do this, I can't do this." We then walked inside and sat down.

At first, we kept the prayers very basic. We had never done a deliverance meeting before, but knew the power of our God and the leading of the Holy Spirit. After ten minutes or so I kept hearing the Holy Spirit say, "Pray for the spirit of addiction to be broken." At first, I tried to justify why it wasn't the right time, but the Spirit of God kept pressing and we started to pray against the spirit of addiction. We gathered around our friend to pray and after about five minutes of this, he started to breathe heavy and make growling sounds. We had no idea what was happening, but kept praying. I then looked directly at my friend and said, "What is your name?" (This was what I read in the Bible and all I knew.) He then looked up, his eyes had turned jet black, and he stated, "Osalge." I then said, "How many demons are in you?" He responded, "289."

At this point all I could think about was the fact that we needed help! We continued to command Osalge to come out and all 289 demons with him. Our friend began to growl louder and breathe heavier and heavier. He then threw himself onto the ground and began to count. I quickly opened the door as we commanded the spirits to leave him and the home. Our friend continued to count, all the way until he reached 289. It then looked like someone punched him in the chest as he fell to the ground.

The room got quiet as we prepared ourselves for round two! He laid on the floor for what seemed like an eternity. To our amazement, he then got up and started to sing in tongues. We looked at one another and questioned what was happening, but he continued to sing and then went to his kitchen and grabbed oil from his cupboard. He went around his house and covered above the entryways with the oil. We all just watched as the act of deliverance was taking place. After 30 minutes or so, he stopped and looked at all of us and asked, "What just happened?" We looked at him and said, "The Spirit of the living God has delivered you." It was around 2:00 AM at this point and our friend who had been tormented by the spirit of addiction for over 10 years had been set free.

What a powerful testimony! To this day, several years later, their friend is free from the addiction that had kept him bound for so long. Addiction is powerful, but there truly is deliverance in the name of Jesus for those who repent and believe.

The Importance of Repentance

I want to make it clear that to acknowledge the influence of evil spirits in situations of bondage and addiction like the testimonies in this chapter does not mean that the person can forfeit responsibility and blame everything on the devil. Bondage to sin happens through a series of choices. There is still a need to take personal responsibility and repent of sin, and there is still a need to overcome the flesh. But in many cases, the possibility of demonic influence is not even considered, leaving people stuck in a hopeless cycle of defeat and shame, with no hope of lasting freedom. So we do not remove the necessity of repentance; we simply add deliverance to the equation when needed.

Repentance and deliverance are actually meant to go hand in hand. When it comes to breaking free from the chains of bondage, repentance is a critical component. A genuine heart of repentance is a precursor to freedom from bondage and demonic influence. We see this truth played out in the Gospel accounts.

It is important to keep in mind that before Jesus came on the scene preaching the Gospel of the Kingdom, healing the sick, and casting out demons, John the Baptist had prepared the way. He called the people to true repentance, to turn from sin and submit to God. He called them to change their mind about sin, break their agreement with it, and bear fruit that demonstrated genuine repentance.

By the time Jesus launched into His ministry, a wave of repentance and revival had swept through Israel through the preaching of John. Jesus continued in this vein, preaching, "Repent, for the kingdom of heaven is at hand" (Matthew 4:17). Jesus came to bring deliverance, but before deliverance came repentance.

The same is true when Jesus sent out the twelve: "So they went out and preached that people should repent. And they cast out many demons" (Mark 6:12-13). First repentance, then deliverance. This order is important. I have found in some cases that people are waiting for God to deliver them, while God is waiting for them to repent. James 4:7 states this same basic concept in a different way: "Therefore submit to God. Resist the devil and he will flee from you." The prerequisite to successfully resisting the devil is being submitted to God. You can try to cast out demons, get delivered, and resist the devil all you want; but if you are not surrendered to God it is all for naught. The degree to which you are submitted to God is the degree to which you can resist the devil.

The primary issue is genuinely desiring freedom, turning your heart to the Lord, and being willing to completely renounce satan and come into agreement with the Word of God. If a person is not serious about being free or not willing to meet God's conditions, it is unlikely that they will be delivered. Some people hate the consequences of being caught in sin, the guilt or shame they feel over it, or the way it impacts their appearance to others. But they have not yet come to the place of godly sorrow that leads to true repentance (see 2 Corinthians 7:10). One of the hardest truths I have had to learn in ministering deliverance is that not everyone truly wants to be free. *You can't get free from the demons that you enjoy company with!*

In dealing with sin issues, Jesus described the need to take drastic measures:

You have heard that it was said, "You shall not commit adultery." But I say to you that everyone who looks at a woman with lustful intent has already committed adultery with her in his heart. If your right eye causes you to sin, tear it out and throw it away. For it is better that you lose one of your members than that your whole body be thrown into hell. And if your right hand causes you to sin, cut it off and throw it away. For it is better that you lose one of your members than that your whole body go into hell (Matthew 5:27-30 ESV).

Obviously, Jesus is not speaking of literally cutting off body parts. He is figuratively describing the heart of a person who is willing to do whatever it takes to be free from the grip of sin. It is not by our own self-effort, but by the grace of God and the power of the cross that we can be free. But we cooperate with the Holy Spirit when we yield in complete repentance and surrender to God. If you are not yet in the place of true repentance and desperation to be free, ask the Holy Spirit to do the work in you to prepare the ground to receive freedom. Call on Jesus to bring you to deeper depths of godly sorrow over sin and genuine heart change. Then, trust Him to break the chains of bondage and set you free.

A Prayer to Break the Chains of Bondage

If you find yourself in the demonic chains of bondage, be encouraged that there is great hope for your freedom. Jesus came to set you free from sin and He has paid the price for your deliverance. Turn to Him in genuine repentance and call on His name.

You can use the following prayer as a guide, but be sure to add your own words and express your heart to God. Fill in the blanks with the specific sins and specific spirits that are relevant to your situation. Take as long as you need and trust the Holy Spirit to lead you.

Father God, I acknowledge that I have sinned against You and others. I come into the light, confessing my sins before You and holding nothing back. I turn my heart to You and ask that You do a deep work of repentance in me. Help me to see sin for what it is and not to justify or minimize it in any way.

I especially confess _____. I repent of all my sins with a desire to live a life pleasing to You. Purify my heart by the power of the blood of Jesus. Right now, I receive Your grace, forgiveness, and cleansing.

By the authority of Jesus' name, I command any unclean spirits related to bondage to sin or addiction to come out. In the name of Jesus, I command the spirit of _____ to leave me right now. I receive freedom from bondage, in Jesus' name!

| 7 |

DELIVERANCE FROM DEMONIC OPPRESSION

I t is always powerful and encouraging to hear stories of captives who have been set free. I often minister deliverance to large groups of people at one time at retreats, conferences, or church services. Many people receive deliverance in these settings, but I will not always know all of the details or hear of the testimonies. It is not uncommon for someone to share with me months or even years later about how they were set free in one of these meetings. Such was the case with Catherine, who told me about her freedom from captivity a year after it had happened.

Catherine had been under a dark depression for several years. She often wrestled with suicidal thoughts and couldn't seem to find relief. One day, she visited a church service where I happened to lead the congregation in a deliverance prayer. At one point I said, "I command the spirit of oppression to come out in Jesus' name!" At that moment, Catherine felt something coming out and lifting off of her. She testified that from that day forward, the depression and suicidal torment was gone. Praise the Lord!

Demonic Oppression

Oppression is one of the characteristic ways that the devil and his demons seek to influence people. When the first martyr, Stephen, was describing how Abraham's descendants would be slaves in Egypt, he said this: "But God spoke in this way: that his descendants would dwell in a foreign land, and that they would bring them into *bondage* and *oppress* them four hundred years" (Acts 7:6). Pharaoh, as a symbolic type of satan, demonstrated two of the ways that evil spirits try to influence people—bondage and oppression. We covered bondage in the previous chapter, and now we will look at oppression.

The apostle Peter, in preaching to the house of Cornelius, summarized the ministry of Jesus like this: "God anointed Jesus of Nazareth with the Holy Spirit and with power, who went about doing good and *healing all who were oppressed by the devil*, for God was with Him" (Acts 10:38). The devil is a cruel oppressor who does not have the capacity for mercy or love. He only comes to steal, kill, and destroy, even though he will often first appear in a deceptive way to lure people into his trap. The more of a stronghold he gets in a person's life, the more he shows himself to be the cruel task-master that he truly is.

The word *oppress* means to exercise harsh control over. Evil spirits seek to weigh people down with heavy burdens—to dominate and harshly control them. Such was the case of the young boy whom Jesus delivered in Mark 9. The father of this boy desperately sought help from the Lord after His disciples were unable to cast out the demon. Check out the description of this demonic oppression: "And wherever it seizes him, it throws him down; he foams at the mouth, gnashes his teeth, and becomes rigid. ...And often he has thrown him both into the fire and into the water to destroy him" (Mark 9:18,22). When Jesus confronted the evil spirit, it cried out, violently convulsed him, and finally came out, leaving the boy looking dead. But Jesus lifted him up by the hand and showed that he was now free from captivity (see Mark 9:25-27).

The Spirit of Heaviness

In Isaiah 61:3 we read that the Messiah will come to give us a "garment of praise for the spirit of heaviness." A *spirit of heaviness* is a demon that seeks to oppress us with hopelessness, depression, and despair. It wants to push us down with burdens and place a dark cloud around us. I have addressed this spirit on many occasions in individuals and in corporate deliverance services.

I was preaching a series of weekend meetings as a guest speaker for a church in the New England area. The pastor had been given my name by a mutual friend and had reached out to me because he believed there was a calling on his church to set captives free. He wanted to see demonic chains of addiction and oppression broken in people's lives, but didn't know where to begin. He believed deliverance was real, but it was not an area that he had much experience in. He invited me to preach and gave me liberty to minister, not knowing exactly how his church would respond to the concept of deliverance from demons.

On the opening night, I preached a message on the central role that deliverance had in the ministry of Jesus. I outlined biblical foundations about demonic influence and how to be set free. I went into a time of corporate ministry, leading the congregation in a prayer for deliverance. I began to command demons to come out from the people and pray as I was led by the Holy Spirit. A young man was highlighted to me by the Lord and I called him out specifically and began to minister to him, addressing the spirit of heaviness and oppression. He immediately dropped to the floor, obviously being touched by the Lord and set free from spiritual chains.

I later found out that this young man had made a last-minute decision to come to the service that night. He had previously left this church and was out of contact with the leadership. But when he and his wife heard about the meeting, they felt compelled to come. His background involved much abuse and trauma, and he had been imprisoned to demonic powers for several years before this break-through moment. God is still delivering people from oppression!

Delivered During Water Baptism

One of my favorite testimonies of deliverance from the devil's oppression happened during a water baptism service that our church hosted. Nyla came to the service to be baptized, but I knew very little about her background. I had met her briefly and had talked to her on the phone about her desire to be baptized. She attended a different church but heard about the baptism service through some friends.

Nyla was born in the Middle East and grew up as a Muslim. Through a series of circumstances, she ended up in the United States as a refugee. Christians began to reach out to her, but at first she was resistant. She eventually went to church with them, and without knowing why she cried throughout the service. God was softening her heart. Jesus soon revealed Himself to her through a vision and a dream, and she committed her life to Him.

There were about 200 people in attendance at the water baptism service. We gathered together at a pond and worshiped God, and then I shared briefly about the significance of being baptized in water. The Holy Spirit had put on my heart that there would be deliverance from evil spirits at this service in connection with water baptism. I had heard of testimonies of deliverance happening during baptism, but had yet to see to see it happen in my own ministry.

I preached from First Corinthians 10:1-2 where the apostle Paul refers to the children of Israel crossing the Red Sea and compares it to baptism. Though the Israelites' redemption was initiated by the blood of the Passover lamb being put on their doorposts, it wasn't until they crossed the Red Sea that their deliverance was complete. In the same way, I explained, water baptism is more than an empty ritual. Though baptism is not what saves us, I believe that there is an actual spiritual transaction that takes place and there is a cutting off of the enemy. I declared that some who had been under demonic influence and oppression would be delivered as they obeyed the Lord in water baptism.

As I began to lead those who were getting baptized in a prayer of declaration of faith in Jesus, Nyla prayed along. But about halfway through the prayer, I noticed that she was no longer praying. She seemed to be in a struggle and had tears running down her face. I discerned that there was a spiritual battle happening in her mind, and took note of it so that I could pray accordingly when she was baptized. (She later told me that during this prayer she was hearing a demon say things like, *What are you doing here? You're going to go to hell if you do this! Go back to Islam! Get out of here!*)

Nyla stepped into the water to be baptized and I laid hands on her and began to pray, breaking off any demonic power and commanding it to go in the name of Jesus. Within seconds, she began to tremble and then let out a long, loud shriek as the demon was cast out of her. She shared later that this demon had been oppressing her for many years, and that nothing would ever help or bring relief. As the demon was leaving, Nyla felt it being torn out of her chest and throat as it screamed in terror at the power of the resurrected Christ!

The crowd of people had witnessed a clear demonstration of the power of God over the kingdom of darkness. For some, this was nothing new, as it is not uncommon for deliverance ministry to happen at our church. But for others, this scene was a little shocking to observe. I had several people ask me about it afterward, wondering what exactly was going on.

The following week, Nyla came to our Sunday morning service and testified about her experience. She explained that she had been oppressed by this demon for many years, from the time she was young. Nothing that she or her parents tried to do would bring any relief, and now it was years later. There was not a dry eye in the crowd as she explained her story in broken English, and testified how Jesus had delivered her in His love and mercy. The place erupted in spontaneous praise to our great God!

Healing the Broken Heart

There is a close connection between the healing of a person's soul and deliverance from captivity. Inner healing and deliverance from demonic oppression are closely related. Let's take another look at one of our main passages of Scripture:

> *The Spirit of the Lord God is upon Me,*
> *Because the Lord has anointed Me*
> *To preach good tidings to the poor;*
> *He has sent Me to **heal the brokenhearted**,*
> *To proclaim **liberty to the captives**,*
> *And the opening of the prison to those who are bound*
> (Isaiah 61:1).

First, it is important to understand that when this passage speaks of bringing good tidings to the *poor* it is not necessarily referring to the financially deprived (although that could also apply). The word in

Hebrew refers to those who are afflicted, downtrodden, or oppressed. Second, notice the flow from healing the brokenhearted to freedom to the captives. These concepts are merged together in this passage and there is a clear relationship between the two.

When this verse speaks of healing the brokenhearted, it is not simply referring to sadness. In the original Hebrew language, this speaks of *binding together a fractured soul*. It refers to a heart that has been shattered, broken, bruised, crushed, or fragmented. Just like our bodies can be injured and broken, so can our heart and mind. This can happen when a person goes through various types of trauma in their life.

Trauma does damage to the interior of a person. And it can also be an open door for demonic oppression. This might not seem fair, but traumatic events create a moment of weakness that can make us more vulnerable to the enemy who "walks about like a roaring lion, seeking whom he may devour" (1 Peter 5:8). The devil doesn't play fair. He is a thief and thieves don't operate by fairness or play by the rules. Traumatic experiences can be the access point that evil spirits use to oppress and torment people. Some examples include fearful accidents, being the victim of a crime, near-death experiences, the sudden death of a loved one, and witnessing violence. Relational betrayal and breakdowns can also become a door that the devil tries to use to oppress people.

Trauma, Abuse, and Demonic Oppression

We must also address the trauma that is related to abuse. One of the main ways I have seen people come under demonic oppression is through experiencing abuse of some kind. This does not just relate to physical harm or violence; it can take on many forms. At its core, abuse is about control and domination over another person in a way that diminishes or destroys their personhood and identity, and violates their will. Whether the abuse is verbal, physical, emotional, sexual, or otherwise, it brings wounding to the interior of a person and often opens the door for evil spirits to harass, oppress, and torment.

I have witnessed the demonic oppression that occurs through abuse:

- When a wife is verbally assaulted and emotionally abused by her husband
- When a young child is sexually violated
- When parental discipline turns into uncontrolled anger and violence
- When word curses are spoken by parents to their children
- When a person is controlled through manipulation and intimidation
- When spiritual authority is misused in order to brainwash and control

Many other scenarios of trauma and abuse could be given. Abuse is pure evil. It is actually satanic in nature, as it takes on the very attributes of the devil who loves to oppress and torment.

When people are recovering from abuse or trauma, I believe that deliverance from evil spirits is often a missing link in the healing process. Counseling is good and helpful, inner healing and the renewal of the mind is needed, and getting grounded in the truths of God's Word is a must. Experiencing God's love in a personal way and connecting with others in loving, healthy relationships is also a part of this journey. But I have seen that many times deliverance from demonic oppression is a critical facet of deep and lasting healing.

God's Heart of Compassion

If you have been wounded by abuse and trauma, or are under demonic oppression in any way, please know that God's heart is toward you. He has a special compassion for the brokenhearted: "The Lord is near to the brokenhearted and saves the crushed in spirit" (Psalm 34:18 ESV). He wants you to experience His love in the depths of your heart and have the weight of oppression lifted from your life.

Jesus modeled this heart of compassion for the afflicted and oppressed throughout His ministry. As I study the life and ministry of Christ, I am struck not only by *what* He did, but by *why* He did it. He would go from place to place preaching the Good News, healing people of their sicknesses, and delivering those who were oppressed. But what motivated Him to do these good works? He was not seeking to build a platform, make a name for Himself, or show off His power. The Gospels give us clear insight into His motives:

> *And when Jesus went out He saw a great multitude; and He was* **moved with compassion** *for them, and healed their sick* (Matthew 14:14).

> *And Jesus, when He came out, saw a great multitude and was* **moved with compassion** *for them...So He began to teach them many things* (Mark 6:34).

Why did Jesus heal the sick and deliver the oppressed? He was moved with compassion for them. Why did He teach the multitudes? He was moved with compassion for them. It was compassion that inspired Jesus to feed the multitudes and raise the dead (see Matthew 15:32; Luke 7:12-15). His whole ministry was motivated by an abundant compassion that flowed out of Him to those around Him. Jesus was not driven by selfish ambition, a desire for power, or an aspiration to be famous. He was compelled by love.

Like Jesus, when we minister to others, it is so important to be moved with God's heart of compassion. Whether it is sharing the Gospel, praying for healing, casting out evil spirits, or meeting needs, we must allow the Lord's love to fill our hearts for the people to whom we minister. Ministry to others is not just about having good answers, saying the right words, or praying the right prayers. First and foremost, it is about having the heart of God.

When I equip people to minister in deliverance, I often share that more important than having the right methods is growing in intimacy with God and compassion for people. All true ministry flows out of relationship with God. And as we grow in intimacy with the Lord, we cannot help but begin to gain His heart for people. This compassion of the Lord flowing through us will often impact people more than the specific ministry that they receive. It communicates God's love to them and makes them know that they are valued, seen, and cared for.

Deliverance is a ministry of compassion to the oppressed. It is a revelation of the heart of God to set captives free out of His mercy and grace. It is not a spiritual power trip, show, or spectacle. It is not about us, but about Jesus and the ones being ministered to. We should be stern and authoritative toward evil spirits but gentle and caring for people receiving ministry. We can grow in our compassion as we ask the Lord to give us His heart for people and yield to the Holy Spirit at work within us. I have found that one of the best ways to grow in compassion is to spend time in the secret place, interceding for people's needs. Allow God to break your heart for things that break His. Don't shy away from feeling His emotions and crying His tears.

We should continually seek God for a greater anointing and power of the Holy Spirit to minister effectively to others. But let's not forget, the Holy Spirit does not come upon us for our own sake, but for the glory of God and the benefit of others. Let's cry out to God to fill us with His heart of love for others. Let's allow His compassion to flow through us so that people can experience God's love in a whole new way.

A Prayer for Deliverance from Oppression

If you are in need of deliverance from oppression, I encourage you to open your heart to God right now and begin to receive His love. His compassion is toward you and He sees what you have been through. He cares about the pain and wants you to be free from demonic oppression.

If you have been through trauma or abuse, it will be important to forgive the ones who hurt you. If necessary, go back and pray through the prayer to forgive others found at the end of Chapter Five.

Take time to pray this prayer, focusing on Jesus and allowing the Holy Spirit to minister to you.

Heavenly Father, I thank You that it is Your desire to heal broken hearts and set captives free. I come to You in the name of Jesus and ask for the Holy Spirit to minister to me on the inside. Fill my heart with Your love. I receive Your love for me in a new way and let go of pain, disappointment, and misunderstanding. I ask to be fully released from any demonic oppression that has come into my life.

In the name of Jesus, I command the spirit of oppression to leave me right now. I rebuke the spirit of heaviness and depression and command it to go from my life. I command any spirits that have come into my life through trauma to come out. I command any spirits that have come in through abuse to leave.

I ask for my heart to be healed and restored, and I receive Your perfect peace. I ask for the oil of joy to be my portion. I

*put on the garment of praise, worshiping and honoring You.
I receive freedom from oppression, in the name of Jesus!*

| 8 |

SET FREE FROM
DEMONIC TORMENT

Now we will look to another area of demonic influence that is
closely related to oppression: torment. I will never forget the
first time that I encountered the *spirit of torment* during a deliverance session. My wife and I were ministering to a young woman
early in our marriage. A demon was manifesting and I commanded it
to name itself. (Jesus did this one time in Mark 5:9. It can be helpful at
times, but I would not recommend it as a regular practice; only when
led by the Holy Spirit.) The woman tilted her head up and looked at
me with a wide-eyed, eerie expression. Out of her mouth, in a voice
not her own, came the word, "Torment!" *Torment* was one of several
spirits that were cast out that evening.

Demons that Torment the Mind

One of the specific ways that demons seek to influence people is to torment and harass. The Gospel of Luke describes people being set free from these types of tormenting spirits: "And He came down with them and stood on a level place with a crowd of His disciples and a great multitude of people from all Judea and Jerusalem, and from the seacoast of Tyre and Sidon, who came to hear Him and be healed of their diseases, *as well as those who were tormented with unclean spirits. And they were healed*" (Luke 6:17-18). Crowds of people came to Jesus from all directions to be healed of sickness and delivered from demonic torment. The Book of Acts records a similar event: "Also a multitude gathered from the surrounding cities to Jerusalem, bringing sick people and those who were *tormented by unclean spirits*, and they were all healed" (Acts 5:16).

The word *tormented* in these passages is *ochleo* in the original Greek language. It means to trouble, harass, vex, torment, or disturb. Demons that aim to torment people often target their attacks in the mind of their victims. Overwhelming and irrational fears, disturbing and intrusive thoughts, accusations and condemnation, feelings of guilt and shame, self-hatred and compulsion toward self-harm, suicidal thoughts—these are all possible ways that evil spirits can seek to torment people.

Many people do not realize that not every thought that enters their mind is their own. The enemy can plant thoughts into our hearts or minds, just as he did with Judas: "The devil having already put it into the heart of Judas Iscariot, Simon's son, to betray Him" (John 13:2). Many times, the tormenting thoughts that people experience are from evil spirits. But because of the lack of understanding in the area of spiritual warfare and deliverance, or for fear of appearing crazy, people do not consider that some of their thoughts can have a demonic origin.

The Occult Brings Torment

One of the ways that tormenting spirits gain access to people's lives is through involvement in the occult. I prayed for a young lady who had spent some time involved in paganism and witchcraft before becoming a believer. She had repented, come to Christ, and left behind her former practices. But she was still struggling with tormenting thoughts and anxiety on a regular basis. She was particularly harassed at night as she tried to sleep. As I prayed over her for deliverance, her countenance would change each time an evil spirit manifested. Her eyes glazed over, and the look on her face changed. Then, when the spirit was cast out, her face would return to normal. She was delivered from multiple demons and left in a place of peace instead of torment.

The word *occult* means "secret" or "hidden" and refers to the supernatural realm of satan. It speaks of secret knowledge into the spirit world, gained through ungodly and illegitimate means. The occult is a broad term that refers to the various activities, groups, and practices that seek knowledge, influence, and power through the spiritual realm outside of the one true living God. There is only one safe way to enter into the supernatural: a relationship with God through Jesus Christ, by the power of the Holy Spirit. Anything outside of this is crossing into spiritual territory that involves demonic deception and influence.

Satan lures people into the occult through deceptive tactics. He makes it look very appealing and attractive; but it always comes with a high price. Some enter into the occult because they have been wounded, and they seek the sense of control or power that is promised. Others are drawn out of mere curiosity or a misguided spiritual hunger for otherworldly things. Some people are born into families that are practitioners of the occult, giving evil spirits access to their lives at a young age. Some are in rebellion and are looking for darkness, while others are actually seeking to do good, but do not know that they are entering into a dark realm. Whether people realize it or not, they are interacting with and welcoming evil spirits into their lives.

I have seen time and again how tormenting spirits have entered into people's lives because they experimented with or got actively involved in occult or New Age activities. When they renounced the occult involvement, the demons were cast out and they were set free from captivity.

(For more information on the occult and how to get free from its influence, see Appendix 2.)

Delivered from the Spirit of Fear

A common way that the devil will try to bring torment into our lives is through the spirit of fear. Fear can be a natural human emotion, but it can also come from a demonic spirit: "For God has not given us a *spirit of fear*, but of power and of love and of a sound mind" (2 Timothy 1:7). When there is crippling anxiety, irrational and tormenting fear, or constant intimidation, there is probably a spirit of fear at work. It has gone beyond natural human fear and into supernatural oppression and torment.

I once preached on overcoming the spirit of fear to a group of young adults. I taught about various aspects of the nature of fear: it is a thief that seeks to rob us of God's promises and our destiny; it is a liar that falsely promises to protect us from the things of which we are afraid; and it is a spirit that seeks to torment us. During the ministry time, I prayed for a young lady who was a visitor to the group that night. Nothing observable or dramatic happened, so it was hard to know if anything significant had taken place. Several months later, I saw her at a friend's birthday party. She reminded me of the night that I had prayed over her to be set free from fear and testified that she had been delivered. The fear that had controlled and bound her was no longer there!

The spirit of fear can come in through a variety of ways. Sometimes it will come when there has been a terrifying or traumatic experience. Sometimes people are exposed to the spirit of fear at a young age through horror movies or scary situations. Sometimes we give in to fear over time and allow the spirit of fear to gain more control in our lives. We should actively resist fear instead of embracing it. We should stand against it because it is an enemy that seeks to hinder us and keep us from our God-given purpose.

Freedom from Anxiety and Depression

Anxiety is a specific form of fear that can paralyze and torment people. After a series of events, a woman named Rachel began to experience depression and anxiety on a daily basis. She lost her best friend in an untimely way to a short battle with cancer. This and other pressures and painful circumstances were beginning to add up, and satan was taking advantage of her situation. Soon, depression began to settle in and anxiety would keep her awake at night.

Rachel began to take her relationship with God more seriously and allow her identity in Christ to be her foundation. She was asking God for healing from anxiety and depression, knowing that this was not His best for her. One day, Rachel's mom was praying for her and God gave her my name. Rachel looked my name up online and found out that I would be ministering at a deliverance service in her area. She and her husband came to the service that night.

After my message, I led the congregation in a prayer for deliverance and began to minister corporately. Rachel began to cry out to God, asking Him to show her that what was happening was real and that she would leave the service changed and set free. Within moments, the Holy Spirit highlighted her to me and I called her out of the crowd, knowing nothing about her situation or what she had just been praying. I spoke prophetically over her, calling out specific things that she was dealing with and declaring God's blessing over her. Tears came down her face as the Lord ministered healing and deliverance to her. From that day forward, the depression and crippling anxiety were gone from her life. She experienced the love of God in a personal way that marked her and allowed her to know that God sees her and cares for her. Praise God that we can be set free from depression, anxiety, and torment, and that we can walk in God's peace.

Do Evil Spirits Impact Mental Health?

The most severe case of demonic torment recorded in the Bible is the man with the legion of demons, found in Mark 5:1-20. The term *legion* implies that there were thousands of demons harassing him. He lived like an animal, naked and among the tombs. People would try to keep him chained, but he would break through the shackles. He was constantly crying out and cutting himself with stones. Today, such a man would be confined in a hospital and considered severely mentally ill. But Jesus addressed the spiritual root of his torment, expelled the legion of demons, and the man was made completely whole in his mind.

This brings up an important question: *could it be that many of the mental health issues that people struggle with today have a demonic element or a spiritual root?* Based on both Scripture and years of practical experience, I certainly believe this to be the case. While there are various factors that can impact an individual's mental health, spiritual torment and oppression certainly need to be factored in as a possibility. We are complex beings made up of body, soul, and spirit. There can be physiological, natural, and emotional reasons for mental health struggles. But we would be naïve to believe that there cannot also be demonic torment at the root of many of these problems.

There is much talk today about suicide prevention and mental health. There seems to be a suicide epidemic and more and more people struggling with anxiety, depression, and other mental health issues. When it comes to how the Church addresses these topics, we cannot leave the spiritual side of things out of the equation.

The vast majority of situations will be much less severe than the man with the legion of demons, but that doesn't mean there aren't things we can learn and apply from his story. Consider the connection to self-destructive behavior: "And always, night and day, he was in the mountains and in the tombs, crying out and cutting himself with stones" (Mark 5:5). Could it be that those today who feel compelled to cut themselves and inflict pain on their own bodies are also being influenced by demonic torment? My experience tells me that this is absolutely the case. It is also significant to note that when the demons left the man and went into a herd of pigs, the pigs exhibited suicidal behavior by running violently off a cliff to drown themselves (see Mark 5:13).

Another story that highlights the connection between demonic influence and self-destructive behavior is found in Mark 9. A father described how a demon drove his son to suicidal behavior: "And often he has thrown him both into the fire and into the water to destroy him" (Mark 9:22). Thankfully, Jesus intervened before the boy could take his own life. I believe that much of the self-destructive and suicidal behavior that we see today has a demonic component. This also applies to other areas such as depression, anxiety, obsessive compulsive disorder, Tourette syndrome, bipolar disorder, and other emotional and mental conditions. While not all mental health issues are automatically the result of demonic torment, I believe that many more are than we realize. We should be open to considering the spiritual side of things and not be afraid or ashamed to acknowledge when deliverance could be needed.

Removing the Stigma from Deliverance

For those who do not understand the ministry of deliverance, it can seem insensitive to suggest that those who have committed suicide may have been tormented by demons. It can seem extreme or careless to imply that self-harm or various mental health issues can be influenced by evil spirits. But when you understand some basics of how demonic influence works—and how common it is—the stigma associated with it is removed. Suggesting that evil spirits can be behind self-destructive behavior and mental illness is not condemning the person who is tormented; it is exposing the activity of demons in order to bring freedom to the tormented.

Whether out of fear, ignorance, or other reasons, the Church has ignored the topic of demons and deliverance for far too long. Belief in the reality of evil spirits is not primitive, superstitious, or foolish; it is perfectly in line with the teachings and example of Christ. Much of the Western culture shuns the idea of demons being the source of torment, oppression, or affliction. But as believers, we must not be ashamed of our supernatural heritage. Instead, we must shine light into the darkness so that more captives can be set free.

If we are to see deliverance embraced by the Church, we must remove the stigma that has so often been attached to it. Because of misunderstanding and fear, many people think that deliverance from an evil spirit sounds alarming, embarrassing, or shameful. Without proper understanding, to suggest that a person might need to be set free from the influence of a tormenting spirit seems insulting or downright crazy. But this stigma need not be the case.

In the New Testament, deliverance from evil spirits was practiced and spoken about openly and plainly. Consider Luke 8:2: "and certain women who had been healed of evil spirits and infirmities—Mary called Magdalene, out of whom had come seven demons." Notice first that being freed from evil spirits is paired side by side with being healed of infirmities. This is often the case in the New Testament (see for example Matthew 8:16-17, Luke 6:17-19, and Acts 5:16). There is no need to be ashamed if you need healing from the flu, the common cold, cancer, or some other disease. In the same way, there is no shame in needing deliverance from evil spirits. Mary Magdalene was identified as someone "out of whom had come seven demons." This was spoken of matter-of-factly, and not something that needed to be kept secret or hidden.

Needing deliverance from evil spirits is not extreme or rare; it is much more common than you might suspect. And to need deliverance from an evil spirit does not make you an evil person. Jesus ministered deliverance to everyday, synagogue-attending Jews like the man in Mark 1 and like the woman He called a "daughter of Abraham" in Luke 13:10-17. Even children needed to be delivered from evil spirits (see Mark 7:24-30 and Mark 9:14-29). As long as we remain ignorant of the enemy's schemes, he has free reign to steal, kill, and destroy. But when we become aware of his activity, we can become equipped to recognize the work of demonic spirits so that we can break free and be empowered to set others free.

A Prayer for Freedom from Torment

As we see the stigma removed from deliverance, we can openly embrace this vital ministry once again in the Western Church. We can include freedom from evil spirits as a factor in issues related to mental torment. We can walk in a biblical, healthy, and balanced approach. We don't have all of the answers, but we should be equipped to address demonic torment and set captives free.

Pray this prayer of deliverance from torment, and ask the Holy Spirit to lead you into greater freedom and peace.

Father, I ask for the Holy Spirit to come and fill my heart with perfect peace. I thank You that You have not given me a spirit of fear, but of power, love, and a sound mind. I thank You that Jesus died on the cross and took the chastisement for my peace.

I renounce any spirits from the kingdom of darkness or any involvement I have had in the occult or New Age. I completely sever all attachments to these practices. Specifically, I renounce

_____.

In the name of Jesus, I command the spirit of torment to come out of me. I command any spirit of fear, anxiety, or intimidation to leave me now, in Jesus' name. I command any spirit of suicide to leave me now. I also command any spirit of confusion to go now, in the name of Jesus.

I receive Jesus as the Prince of Peace in my life. I receive healing in my heart and mind, and commit my thoughts to the Lord. Thank You for freedom from torment!

| 9 |

FREEDOM FROM THE SPIRIT OF INFIRMITY

I went to Donna's house at the request of a mutual friend. When I walked in the door, I saw a woman who looked like *death*. Her skin was pale and her countenance displayed oppression. I talked to her and her husband for a while, getting the backstory to her situation. Doctors had diagnosed her with multiple conditions, including Lyme disease, but her illness was still somewhat of a mystery. Her mobility was severely limited; she was sometimes confined to a wheelchair, and could not walk upstairs without severe pain. Her physical condition was a major source of stress for the family, as it impaired her ability to run their at-home business and hindered her capacity to mother their children.

As I asked questions and gathered information, it became apparent that this condition was more than physical. Donna had grown up in a family where her father was a practicing warlock. This, among other things, had opened the door to demonic influence. I explained to the couple what deliverance is and we talked through what the Bible teaches about the reality of evil spirits causing physical affliction. They agreed to try a prayer of deliverance.

When Donna prayed through the prayer, there were some mild demonic manifestations that occurred and she also wept as she received some emotional healing. After some time of ministry, I asked her to walk around to see if she felt any different from before. She began to walk around the house and then came to the true test—the stairs. She started to walk up the steps freely, something she had not been able to do for a long time. When she got to the top of the steps she began to weep for joy. There was no pain!

I followed up the next day to see how she was doing. She reported that she had been able to drive and run errands with her children for the first time in a while, and that the symptoms of pain and sickness were continuing to disappear. Praise God for His healing grace!

The Connection Between Healing and Deliverance

When we read the New Testament accounts, we can see that physical healing and deliverance from demons are very closely related. Though there is a distinction between these two ministries, there is also much overlap. Healing ministry primarily refers to the restoration of the physical body back to health by the power of the Holy Spirit. Deliverance refers to casting out evil spirits to free people from various types of demonic influence. But as we will see, these two ministries go hand in hand.

Consider the following examples from the Gospel of Luke:

> *When the sun was setting, all those who had any that were sick with various diseases brought them to Him; and He*

laid His hands on every one of them and healed them. And demons also came out of many... (Luke 4:40-41).

...and a great multitude of people...who came to hear Him and be healed of their diseases, as well as those who were tormented with unclean spirits. And they were healed. And the whole multitude sought to touch Him, for power went out from Him and healed them all (Luke 6:17-19).

And that very hour He cured many of infirmities, afflictions, and evil spirits; and to many blind He gave sight (Luke 7:21).

And certain women who had been healed of evil spirits and infirmities—Mary called Magdalene, out of whom had come seven demons (Luke 8:2).

There are many other biblical examples that could be given, but the examples above provide clear evidence of the relationship between healing and deliverance. Healing of sickness and deliverance from demons are mentioned in the same breath. These ministries are meant to go together and often intersect. In the ministry of Jesus, healing and deliverance were the two most common supernatural signs. They were a demonstration of the message that Jesus preached—the Kingdom of Heaven is at hand. As the Kingdom of God advanced, healing the sick and casting out demons were by-products.

Sometimes Jesus healed people by laying hands on them or speaking a word of command to them. Other times, healing was a direct result of a demon being cast out. The New Testament is clear that evil spirits can cause sickness. On the flip side, I have seen that sometimes a traumatic or prolonged physical sickness can be a door opener for evil spirits to gain entrance. You never know when healing will turn into deliverance or deliverance into healing. This means that if we want to grow in healing ministry, we should also be familiar with deliverance. And if we want to grow in deliverance, we should also be growing in healing. Though they are distinct and can be done independently of each other, they are so closely related that we should not completely isolate them from one another.

I remember the first time I experienced the clear connection between healing and deliverance many years ago. I was praying for a young lady who was having neck pain. I prayed over her for healing, but nothing happened. The following week, she asked for prayer to receive deliverance. She was aware that there were demonic spirits tormenting her and pressuring her toward sin. Another woman and I prayed over her, and several demons manifested and were cast out. Interestingly, the pain in her neck was totally healed, even though we had not addressed it specifically. Evidently, it had been caused by an evil spirit, and once the spirit was cast out the pain was gone.

Just as emotional healing and deliverance are closely linked, so are physical healing and deliverance. And through the cross, Jesus has paid the price for our healing and wholeness in every area.

The Spirit of Infirmity

In the previous several chapters we looked at how evil spirits can cause bondage, oppression, and torment. But another characteristic activity of demons is to afflict people with sickness and disease. Surely, many medical doctors today would laugh at the notion that evil spirits are the cause of a physical ailment or a mental disorder. But it is satan who is laughing while he goes unnoticed bringing torment and sickness to people. The Bible is our source of truth. Even if many doctors, psychologists, scientists, and even pastors scoff at the idea of evil spirits causing sickness, we must examine the Scriptures to see what they teach in this area. Though there have been great medical and scientific advances, if we see sickness only from a natural standpoint, we will often miss the root cause of the problem.

One of the primary examples of an evil spirit being the root of a physical affliction comes from Luke 13:

> *Now He was teaching in one of the synagogues on the Sabbath. And behold, there was a woman who had a spirit of infirmity eighteen years, and was bent over and could in no way raise herself up. But when Jesus saw her, He called her to Him and said to her, "Woman, you are loosed from your infirmity." And He laid His hands on her, and immediately she was made straight, and glorified God. But the ruler of the synagogue answered with indignation, because Jesus had healed on the Sabbath; and he said to the crowd, "There are six days on which men ought to work; therefore come and be healed on them, and not on the Sabbath day." The Lord then answered him and said, "Hypocrite! Does not each one of you on the Sabbath loose his ox or donkey from the stall, and lead it away to water it? So ought not this woman, being a daughter of Abraham, whom satan has bound—think of it— for eighteen years, be loosed from this bond on the Sabbath?" And when He said these things, all His adversaries were put to shame; and all the multitude rejoiced for all the glorious things that were done by Him* (Luke 13:10-17).

The woman in the synagogue was crippled in her spine, having a condition that today would probably be diagnosed as a severe form of scoliosis. But the cause of this problem is clearly stated: a *spirit of infirmity.* Her physical condition had a spiritual root. Jesus spoke a word of healing to her and then laid His hands on her. The woman was healed immediately. Notice that when the ruler of the synagogue complained about this healing happening on the Sabbath, Jesus referred to the woman as a daughter of Abraham whom *satan had kept bound.* She had not merely been dealing with a physical ailment; she had been in captivity to the evil one.

The New Testament has other relevant examples as well. Matthew 9:32-33 reads: "As they went out, behold, they brought to Him a man, mute and demon-possessed. And when the demon was cast out, the mute spoke." Here we have a man who was mute, and the clear cause of the condition was a demon. Jesus later healed a man who was both blind and mute by casting out a demon (see Matthew 12:22). In Matthew 17 Jesus healed a young boy who suffered from epileptic seizures. Verse 18 states, "And Jesus rebuked the demon, and it came out of him; and the child was cured from that very hour." The source of the boy's sickness was an evil spirit that needed to be cast out in order for him to be healed.

Just like in the New Testament, I have personally seen various types of physical afflictions healed through the casting out of demons. Not all sickness, disease, or pain is caused by a demon. There can be natural causes and various factors involved. But I believe it is much more common than we often realize for evil spirits to be the source of an affliction. We must not allow modern cultural influences to cloud out the clear biblical truth in this area. Let's ask for greater discernment to recognize when a spirit of infirmity is at work, and a greater anointing to heal the afflicted.

Delivered from the Spirit of Death

There is a demon called the *spirit of death*. This is a spirit that seeks to bring terminal sickness, premature death, or tormenting fear of death. It works together with the spirit of infirmity to increase the affliction in a person's life.

I shared in a previous chapter about a young lady to whom my wife and I ministered, who was having recurring intrusive thoughts of death. She would be driving her car and suddenly she would imagine herself drifting off the road, crashing, and dying. During her teenage years, she had overcome an extended battle with cancer. It was a few years later and she was now cancer free, but was still battling thoughts of death.

I have found that the spirit of death can come in sometimes during major and prolonged sicknesses. When a person is continually faced with the real possibility of death, it can be a traumatic experience. The dark spirit of death can seek to gain a place of influence during these times. It can settle in and hover over a person's mind, trying to gain a stronghold of fear and torment.

My wife and I led the young woman in a prayer for deliverance and commanded demons to leave. There was resistance at first, but the Holy Spirit broke through and she was powerfully delivered. Not only was she set free from the spirit of death, but several other demons as well. And on top of that, God also completely healed her of a stomach problem that she had been suffering from for three years due to her prior cancer treatments. Her stomach lining had been damaged and she often experienced discomfort and nausea. There was such an atmosphere of the power of God in the room that we had a strong expectation for her to be healed. My wife laid hands on her stomach and we both prayed. There was a gift of faith to declare a new stomach, and her mid-section began to vibrate. She was healed that day and hasn't had the stomach problems since. We serve a miracle-working God!

This testimony is a great example of the connection between healing and deliverance. As this young woman fought through the battle with cancer, it became an open door for unclean spirits to take advantage of her situation and bring affliction and torment. Though she physically recovered through the medical treatments, she remained in a condition of oppression afterward. When she was delivered from the unclean spirits, there was also healing released for her stomach. Deliverance and healing were intertwined together.

Breakthrough in Healing

I believe that as the Church embraces the ministry of deliverance on a broader scale, we will also see a greater breakthrough in physical healing. I was once drawn to the progression of the ministry of Philip the evangelist in Samaria. Read the following verses, considering the order of what is outlined:

> *Then Philip went down to the city of Samaria and preached Christ to them. And the multitudes with one accord heeded the things spoken by Philip, hearing and seeing the miracles which he did. **For unclean spirits, crying with a loud voice, came out of many who were possessed; and many who were paralyzed and lame were healed**. And there was great joy in that city* (Acts 8:5-8).

Philip came into a region that was once under the spiritual control of a sorcerer named Simon (see Acts 8:9-10). Philip's message was centered on Jesus and the Kingdom of God, while Simon's message was about glorifying himself. Simon worked supernatural magic through occultic power, while Philip's message was accompanied by demonstrations of miraculous power through the Holy Spirit and the name of Jesus. This was a clash of kingdoms, a supernatural show-down. God's power prevailed and multitudes in the city of Samaria turned to the Lord.

Notice the order of the miraculous signs mentioned: first it says that many were delivered from unclean spirits. Then it says that many were healed of debilitating physical ailments. I believe there is a key for greater breakthrough in healing in this text. If we will embrace and establish the ministry of deliverance, we will also see a greater increase in the realm of physical healing. The two go closely together, and work together in tandem.

Is It Natural or Spiritual?

We have already seen various biblical examples of a physical infirmity being the direct result of the influence of an evil spirit. Jesus often healed the sick by casting out demons. But there are plenty of other examples where people received healing without any mention of casting out evil spirits. Jesus healed a blind man by putting mud on his eyes and telling him to wash in a pool (see John 9:1-7). In some cases, He healed the mute by casting out demons, and in other cases He simply made commands for deaf ears to be opened (see Luke 11:14; Mark 7:31-35). The woman with the issue of blood was healed by reaching up and touching the hem of His garment (see Mark 5:25-29). There are various other examples that could be given, but the point is clear. Sometimes sickness has direct demonic involvement and other times it does not.

This again demonstrates the continual need for spiritual discernment. Is the sinful habit a person is stuck in a work of the flesh, or does it also involve demonic bondage? Is the mental health issue a person is facing physiological, or does it contain demonic oppression and spirits of torment? Does the physical health problem someone is fighting have purely a natural cause, or is there a spirit of infirmity that needs to be addressed? These are all great questions and we should walk in a healthy perspective and have a balanced approach. Not all problems are caused by demons, but many problems are. It is a lazy approach to discernment to make all things demonic on one hand, or nothing demonic on the other. With either of those extremes, there is no need to actually discern on a case-by-case basis. The fact is, each situation is unique and we always need God's wisdom and guidance. And many cases involve multiple factors.

Aside from supernatural discernment from the Holy Spirit or a demonic manifestation indicating the presence of an evil spirit, how can we determine if a sickness has a demonic component? Here are a few signs that indicate a stronger probability of there being a spiritual root:

- When you receive prayer for healing, pain increases or moves around in your body.
- There is mystery surrounding the physical symptoms, and doctors struggle to find a diagnosis.
- The physical symptoms are related to trauma or abuse that was experienced.
- It is considered an incurable disease.
- There is unforgiveness in your life that has opened the door to affliction.

Prayer of Deliverance from Infirmity

If you are in need of healing, or simply want to pray for your body to be in better health, pray along with this prayer below.

Lord Jesus, I thank You that You are the same yesterday, today, and forever. You are still the Healer and the One who sets captives free. I thank You that You took stripes on Your back for my healing and restoration. I look to You and ask for Your Holy Spirit to come upon me and quicken my body with strength and health.

I rebuke all sickness and disease and command it to leave me in the name of Jesus. I rebuke the spirit of infirmity, pain, and sickness and command these spirits to come out of me right now. I command the spirit of death to leave me now, in Jesus' name.

I receive healing, health, and the abundant life that Jesus came to give me!

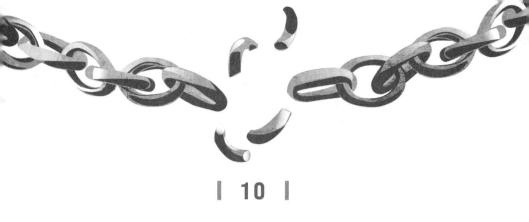

I 10 I

UPROOTING GENERATIONAL CURSES AND STRONGHOLDS

In the past several chapters, we have covered various specific areas of demonic influence. Bondage to sin and destructive behaviors, oppression and spiritual heaviness, torment in the mind, and physical affliction and infirmity are some of the main ways that demons seek to have a hold in people's lives.

We will now deal with the topic of uprooting generational curses and strongholds. The subject of generational curses can be controversial and confusing, and I hope that this chapter will bring some insight and clarity. It is important to understand the nature of generational curses because they can be an open door to demonic influence and can impact various areas of a person's life. We shouldn't make a formula out of this, but I have found that for some people, breaking a generational curse was a key part of their journey to freedom.

What Is a Curse?

Though the idea of a curse may seem primitive or superstitious to our Western minds, the concept of blessings and curses is mentioned frequently throughout the Bible. In the Scriptures, we see examples of God's blessing being a tangible reality, bringing fruitfulness, abundance, and protection to His people. We see how the spoken blessing of a father or priest was taken very seriously and sought after. We also see how curses could come to God's people through disobedience or idolatry, and how they brought destruction, sickness, and lack.

A curse can be defined as *a supernatural force in a person's life that brings harm or keeps them from receiving God's blessings.* Curses are often empowered by evil spirits, which gives them supernatural power that needs to be broken. Some of the possible symptoms that a curse is at work are:

- A continual inability to move forward in life
- A dark cloud of oppression that doesn't seem to budge
- Destructive or sinful behaviors that run in the family
- A constant sense of frustration
- Patterns of inexplicable sickness or accidents
- Continuous financial lack and instability
- A cycle of relational breakdowns
- An inability to conceive or a pattern of miscarriages
- A sense of an unseen barrier between you and God

Please note that the presence of one or more of these does not automatically always mean that a curse is in place. They are simply possible signs that should be prayed through and explored to determine whether something beneath the surface is at work, beyond natural explanation.

Proverbs 26:2 says this: "Like a flitting sparrow, like a flying swallow, so a curse without cause shall not alight." This indicates that every curse has a cause; that a curse cannot be present if there is not a reason for it to be there or something that caused it to "land" on a person. Curses can come because of disobedience, idolatry, and occult involvement. They can be released against us through others' words or through the practice of witchcraft. And generational sin and iniquity is also one of the causes of curses. As we explore this topic, keep in mind that a Christian does not have to remain under any curse. Part of Christ's work of redemption was to become a curse for us so that we could be delivered from every curse and receive God's blessing.

> *Christ has redeemed us from the curse of the law, having become a curse for us* (for it is written, "Cursed is everyone who hangs on a tree"), *that the blessing of Abraham might come upon the Gentiles in Christ Jesus, that we might receive the promise of the Spirit through faith* (Galatians 3:13-14).

As with deliverance, breaking curses is an act that enforces what Jesus has already accomplished for us through His death and resurrection. He has paid the price to set us free from every curse!

Generational Curses

In a symbolic reference to defeating the Amorites—an enemy nation—the Lord said this to Israel: "I destroyed his fruit above and his roots beneath" (Amos 2:9). There is a principle enclosed in this brief statement: if there is fruit above, then there are roots beneath. Fruit in our lives—both good and bad—does not grow overnight. Before fruit can be produced there must be roots beneath the surface. For the sake of our study here, I want to apply this to sinful behaviors and negative characteristics.

In dealing with sinful behavior and negative characteristics, it is important that we deal with not only the behavior itself, but also the root cause. Like God dealt with the Amorites, we must destroy both the fruit above and the roots beneath. If you have ever pulled weeds, you know that if you do not deal with the roots, the weed will spring back up in no time. It is the same with the bad fruit in our lives. We need to cut out the root so that the fruit will not be able to grow.

What does this have to do with generational curses? A generational curse is an example of a root beneath the surface that produces bad fruit above the surface. A generational curse is simply a curse or stronghold that is passed down from one generation to the next. Just like we receive an inheritance of physical traits from our parents, we also receive a spiritual inheritance from our family line. This includes both blessings and curses. One of the foundational Scriptures for this is Exodus 20:4-6:

> You shall not make for yourself a carved image—any likeness of anything that is in heaven above, or that is in the earth beneath, or that is in the water under the earth; you shall not bow down to them nor serve them. For I, the Lord your God, am a jealous God, visiting the iniquity of the fathers upon the children to the third and fourth generations of those who hate Me, but showing mercy to thousands, to those who love Me and keep My commandments.

The iniquity of parents is visited upon their children. To be clear, this does not mean that children are charged with guilt for the sins of their parents (see Deuteronomy 24:16 and Ezekiel 18:19-20). However, the sins of parents do have an adverse effect upon their children and open the door for similar patterns of sin. When parents—who are meant to provide spiritual protection for their children—walk in iniquity, idolatry, and sin, children are left more vulnerable to the enemy's work. As the sin of Adam and Eve passed on to their offspring, so our sinful tendencies can pass on to our offspring.

Sinful Strongholds Passed Down

Have you ever wondered why some people are prone to certain sins while others are not? There are various factors that can influence this, but one of them is generational curses. Sinful strongholds that are not broken end up being passed down to the next generation. If there is a pattern of sexual sin in your family line, this may be a bigger battle for you than for others. If one of your parents couldn't conquer uncontrollable anger, you may find that you are also prone to outbursts of rage. The same could be said of worry, greed, unbelief, pride, or various other types of sin.

We can see examples of this dynamic in Scripture. While Abraham is considered the father of the faith and had a tremendous walk with God, he had his sins and flaws like the rest of us. One time he used deception to protect himself before a king, asking Sarah to lie about being his wife and to claim only to be his sister. What is fascinating is that Abraham's son, Isaac, fell into this exact same trap. And then we know that Isaac's son, Jacob, had a problem with using deception. We can see that this pattern of sin was passed from one generation to the next.

The following testimony illustrates how freedom from a generational curse can be an important aspect of deliverance from bondage. A young man named Steve had been pulled into sexual fantasy and immorality at a very young age. He found himself drawn to it, even before he was ever exposed to pornography. This only increased as he got older. He was involved in pornography, and after getting married this continued to be a problem. He was tempted toward infidelity and seemed to be stuck in a pattern of immorality. He attended a weekend conference that I spoke at on the topic of deliverance. On the opening night he experienced a demonic manifestation while in the meeting, and knew that he needed to come the next day to receive ministry. During the prayer for deliverance on that next day, he began to experience more manifestations, particularly when we were breaking generational curses. He was delivered that day, and has never been the same since. The drawing to sexual immorality has been broken and he is walking in freedom and purity.

This shows how a generational curse can be the root cause of a sinful pattern and how breaking the curse can be a key for finding lasting freedom. To be clear, we can never blame our parents or previous generations for our own choices and sins. We must take responsibility and repent where we have sinned. But being able to identify generational curses and strongholds can help explain why we battle certain sins more than others and can help us get free. We can receive deliverance from sinful strongholds and any evil spirits that are attached to them, and we can begin to walk in the blessing of God. And we are not just fighting for ourselves; we are fighting for future generations. What we conquer, our children will inherit!

Delivered from Generational Affliction

One of the types of generational curses relates to physical infirmities and mental illnesses. What is the first thing that happens when you go to the doctor's office? They have you fill out a form that outlines your family's medical history. Doctors know that certain types of diseases have a tendency to pass on through the family line. But what they may not recognize is that this pattern can actually be a spiritual problem, not just a genetic one. While not every sickness is the result of a curse, sickness, disease, and mental torment are all included in the list of curses that are outlined in Scripture (see Deuteronomy 28:20-22, 27-28, 58-61). Deuteronomy 28:59 speaks specifically of plagues coming upon "you and your descendants," showing the generational impact.

Diseases such as cancer and heart disease; mental health issues of depression, bi-polar disorder, and anxiety; problems with barrenness or miscarriages—these can all be passed through the family line and be inherited. God's heart for His children is not for sickness, disease, or mental torment to afflict them. His heart is to bless and to heal, but the consequences of the Fall and the personal sins of people have opened the way for all types of destruction and death in the world. Being aware of the reality of generational sickness and disease should not scare us but equip us to receive healing if what we are dealing with is a generational curse.

I was preaching at a conference in Florida, and in one of my sessions I did a teaching on breaking free from generational curses and strongholds that have been passed down through the family line. At the end of the teaching, I led the congregation in a prayer to receive deliverance from curses and step into greater freedom. About a week later, I received a message from a lady who had attended the meeting. For seven years, she had suffered from debilitating headaches and was constantly taking medicine to relieve the pain. As she prayed through the prayer during the ministry time, it occurred to her that both her father and grandfather suffered from similar problems with headaches.

When she awoke the next morning, she could not find her pain killers and so she went without them. As the day went on, she realized that she was not experiencing any headaches, so she went the whole day without medicine. This continued for the whole week until she realized that she had been completely healed; no more headaches! Through the breaking of a generational curse, she was delivered from the physical torment she had been under for many years.

Occult and Secret Societies

The Exodus passage that was quoted earlier in this chapter speaks specifically about the sin of idolatry causing generational iniquity. Idolatry relates to the worship of anything other than the one true living God. This can happen in the traditional sense of the worship of physical idols, but idolatry is much broader than this. The Bible speaks of setting up idols in the heart and also equates covetousness with idolatry (see Ezekiel 14:3 and Colossians 3:5). Even good things can become idols if we allow them to take the place of God. We are to ascribe to God the highest worth and give Him our love and devotion above all else.

A specific type of idolatry to be aware of is involvement in the occult or secret societies. Many types of participation in occult practices and secret societies require you to take oaths and curses, and even commit your children to these curses. Idolatry and occult involvement are iniquities that are visited upon the family line and passed from one generation to the next. These curses can take the form of an overshadowing darkness over a person's life, unexplainable sickness and pain, a drawing to spiritual darkness, or other destructive patterns.

Doug had experienced an unusual series of difficulties for several years and was unable to find breakthrough. A friend of his shared a sermon that I had preached on breaking generational curses. He listened to it one day during a long drive, and as the message began he felt a tingling sensation and chill go through his body. His father was a Freemason and had actually introduced Doug into the orientation process. When he got to a part in the message where I mentioned Freemasonry, he was hit with the realization that he had been carrying the Mason membership card in his wallet for the previous several years.

As he continued to listen to the message, he began to have a demonic manifestation. He was yelling and screaming at top of his lungs and had a huge ringing in his ears. As the message transitioned into a ministry time, he began to cough violently and actually saw a demonic face on his windshield. When he got to his friend's house, he asked her to pray over him while he burned the Mason card. He had never even heard about deliverance until he experienced it that day!

Destructive Behaviors and Faulty Mindsets

Similar to sinful patterns, destructive behaviors can be passed through the family line. You can often see cycles of harmful tendencies going from one generation to the next. Suicidal inclinations and self-harm can go from parents to children. Abuse of all kinds can end up passing through a family line for generations. Addictions to alcohol and drugs can run in the family. Patterns of marital breakdown and divorce can be traced through a lineage. The enemy comes to steal, kill, and destroy; and he not only wants to lay hold of individuals, but also to get a stronghold in whole family lines.

Destructive generational behaviors can usually be obvious to identify, but faulty mindsets can be subtler. For example, religious strongholds of legalism and traditionalism can be passed down. Consider Stephen's rebuke to the religious leaders of his day: "You stiff-necked and uncircumcised in heart and ears! You always resist the Holy Spirit; *as your fathers did, so do you*" (Acts 7:51). There was a generational resistance to hearing God's voice and allowing the Holy Spirit to work. There were traditions passed from one generation to the next that opposed the work of God, even though they were religious in nature.

Mindsets of condemnation, perfectionism, skepticism and unbelief, judgmental attitudes, and other unhealthy strongholds can flow through the family line.

Breaking Generational Curses

Some people are in the battle of their lives because they are the transition point in a family line. They are breaking destructive cycles and sinful strongholds that have been passed on from generation to generation. They are uprooting these curses and establishing a new legacy for generations to come. This can be a difficult and fierce battle at times, because you are working against the years of history and working toward a future legacy. You are not just fighting for yourself, you are fighting for your children, grandchildren, and many generations to come!

Though Christ provided freedom for us from generational curses, this does not mean that they all automatically go away when a person becomes a believer. Remember that through the cross Christ also provided freedom from the power of sin and healing from sickness, but these are not necessarily fully received when someone comes to Christ in salvation. In the same way, it is often necessary to specifically pray through and break free from the influence of generational curses and strongholds. The following steps can be a helpful guide to walk you through this process.

1. Recognize the provision of the cross.

First and foremost, we must recognize that it is through the finished work of Jesus that we receive deliverance from all curses. This is a part of what Jesus purchased for us on the cross. Let's look again at Galatians 3:13-14: "Christ has redeemed us from the curse of the law, having become a curse for us (for it is written, 'Cursed is everyone who hangs on a tree'), that the blessing of Abraham might come upon the Gentiles in Christ Jesus, that we might receive the promise of the Spirit through faith." Jesus became a curse for us so that we could be delivered from every curse. This is good news! No Christian needs to live under the effect of a curse, including generational curses.

Just as we look to Jesus for forgiveness, healing, and freedom from evil spirits, we look to Him to break us free from destructive patterns that have been passed on through our family line.

2. *Renounce the sins of previous generations.*

If you are aware of specific strongholds of sin, occult activity, idolatry, cycles of sickness, or other generational influences, make sure to pray through them by name. You can pray something like this, filling in the blank with the specific sins, strongholds, and curses of your family line:

> *Lord Jesus, thank You for dying on the cross and becoming a curse so that I could be redeemed from every curse and receive God's blessing. Because of Your finished work, I ask You to set me free from every curse that is over my life. I renounce the sins of previous generations and break away from any generational curse that is over my life. Specifically, I break free from _____. I repent for any ways that I have participated in these sinful patterns. I declare that the blood of Jesus separates me from the sins and curses of my family line.*

When you pray this prayer, you should also command any evil spirits that have been inherited through your generational line to come out in the name of Jesus. You might be surprised at what happens!

3. *Receive the blessings of being a child of God.*

Notice that in the Galatians 3:13-14 passage quoted, the work does not end with deliverance from the curse; it ends with inheriting "the blessing of Abraham" and receiving the "promise of the Spirit." On the basis of what Jesus has accomplished for us, we receive and walk in the blessing of God. We do not have to be subject to the strongholds and sins of previous generations. We are new creations in

Christ—old things have passed away and all things are made new (see 2 Corinthians 5:17).

Let's take our stand in Christ to walk free from the strongholds and demonic influences that may have come through our family line. And the great thing is, we now get to pass on generational blessings to our children!

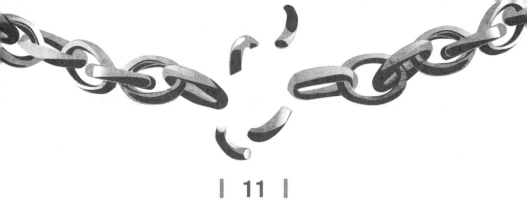

| 11 |

BREAKING WORD CURSES AND SEVERING SOUL TIES

was speaking at a deliverance seminar and part of my teaching covered breaking the power of word curses. I began to describe the power of words either to bless or to curse, and how words can be demonically inspired and have an assignment from the enemy. As I was sharing this, a man sitting near the front named Daniel began to cry. I could tell that something was being stirred up. During the ministry time, he came forward for prayer and was delivered as someone from the ministry team prayed for him. After the meeting, he shared his story with me.

Daniel had been a pastor for several years, but his church went through some turmoil and tension on the leadership team, and he eventually left. During this time, the man who took his place as pastor spoke slanderous words about Daniel publicly. God revealed to Daniel during my teaching that those words were a curse, and he was set free from the demonic assignment that came with the false accusations and slander.

The Power of Words

The Bible teaches that our words are very important and that they carry power. I believe that this is one of the ways in which human beings have been created in the image of God. Just like the heavens and the earth were created as God spoke, God has endowed us with the power of words, and this can be used as a tremendous blessing to others. I am aware that teaching on the power of words can be taken to unscriptural extremes, making it seem like we can have and do whatever we want as long as we just say the right words. This teaching is more like "charismatic magic" than true biblical prayer and declaration. Nonetheless, the power of words is a biblical concept. Our words are obviously not on the same level as God's, but they are indeed powerful.

Consider what Paul wrote to the Ephesians: "Let no corrupt word proceed out of your mouth, but what is good for necessary *edification*, that it may *impart grace* to the hearers" (Ephesians 4:29). Think about this: our words have the capacity to edify, or build people up, and to actually impart grace to others. It strikes me as significant that one of the means by which God has ordained grace to be released in our lives is through the words of other believers. And we can yield our words to the Lord in such a way that they release grace to others—how awesome!

When Words Become Curses

Our words can release blessing, comfort, and grace, but unfortunately it is also possible for corrupt words to flow from our mouths. Just like words can be used to release life and blessing, they can also be used to release terrible damage into people's lives. With our words we can tear down, belittle, accuse, lie, slander, gossip, criticize, and demean. Proverbs 18:21 indicates that our words can either bring forth life or bring forth death: "Death and life are in the power of the tongue, and those who love it will eat its fruit." And consider the strong and descriptive language that James uses in describing the evil that can come from the tongue:

> *And the tongue is a fire, a world of iniquity. The tongue is so set among our members that it defiles the whole body, and sets on fire the course of nature; and it is set on fire by hell. For every kind of beast and bird, of reptile and creature of the sea, is tamed and has been tamed by mankind. But no man can tame the tongue. It is an unruly evil, full of deadly poison. With it we bless our God and Father, and with it we curse men, who have been made in the similitude of God. Out of the same mouth proceed blessing and cursing. My brethren, these things ought not to be so* (James 3:6-10).

We don't have the power to tame our tongues, but the Holy Spirit certainly does. The tongue untamed by the Lord and unyielded to the Holy Spirit can be set on fire by hell and release lethal poison to its hearers. The same mouth that can release blessing can also place curses on people; and James is giving this warning to believers!

When the Bible mentions the idea of curses proceeding from our mouths, it is not referring merely to filthy language (which should certainly be avoided), but to words spoken that carry spiritual power to actually become a curse in a person's life. We have all heard the old saying, "Sticks and stones may break my bones, but words will never hurt me," but this couldn't be further from the truth. The reality is, words can do devastating harm. They can pierce our soul like a sword and poison us like a serpent's bite (see Proverbs 12:18 and Psalm 140:3). Many people are still living under the effect of destructive words that were spoken to them years ago. These types of words are referred to as a *word curse*.

A word curse is a statement that is spoken over someone in such a way as to create a curse on their life. (Remember that in the previous chapter we defined a curse as a supernatural force in a person's life that brings harm or keeps them from receiving God's blessings.) This typically (but not always) happens when the one speaking is a person of authority or significant influence in the other person's life—for example, a parent, teacher, sibling, spouse, boss, or pastor. These statements are spoken as authoritative facts, and although they are most often not intended as a literal curse, when they are believed and received they become a curse over the life of the one who hears them.

Probably the best way to explain word curses is to give some examples. Below are some samples of negative declarations that can become a curse in the life of a child when they are spoken by a mother or father:

- "You are so stupid! You are never going to amount to anything in life."
- "You are going to end up just like your father" (in a negative sense).
- "You are such a failure. Can't you do anything right?"
- "Nobody would ever want to marry you."
- "You'd be better off locked up in jail."
- "You always get into accidents. You're such a klutz!"
- "You are such a pain! All you do is cause trouble."

These types of statements do terrible damage to the soul of a child. They get attached to their identity and become intertwined with who they are. When statements like this are accepted as true, the person begins to live up to the expectations created by the word curses, and an invisible barrier keeps them from moving beyond the hurtful words. Curses like this are often empowered by an evil spirit who reinforces the lies that have been spoken.

Destructive Words and Demonic Influence

Just as our words can be edifying to others, they can also be *destructive* in nature. Our words are not meant to be evil or corrupt, but to build others up and impart grace to them, as we saw earlier: "Let no corrupt word proceed out of your mouth, but what is good for necessary edification, that it may impart grace to the hearers" (Ephesians 4:29). But the enemy wants to use our words as weapons of destruction. He comes to steal, kill, and destroy; and reckless and destructive words are one of his choice weapons.

> *With his mouth the godless man would **destroy** his neighbor, but by knowledge the righteous are **delivered*** (Proverbs 11:9 ESV).

Notice that godless words are destructive, and that through knowledge we can be delivered from their influence. We must know the truth and learn to discern when we are under demonic attack through the harmful words of another person. We must also understand that destructive words like slander, false accusations, and cursing do not merely cause discouragement. They can actually do great damage to our soul. Consider the following verses:

> *The words of the wicked lie in wait for blood...* (Proverbs 12:6 ESV).
> *A worthless man plots evil, and his speech is like a scorching fire* (Proverbs 16:27 ESV).
> *There is one whose rash words are like sword thrusts, but the tongue of the wise brings healing* (Proverbs 12:18 ESV).

Hide me from the secret plots of the wicked, from the rebellion of the workers of iniquity, who sharpen their tongue like a sword, and bend their bows to shoot their arrows—bitter words, that they may shoot in secret at the blameless; suddenly they shoot at him and do not fear (Psalm 64:2-4).

Notice the types of things that godless and destructive words are compared to—murderous ambush, a scorching fire, being stabbed with a sword, and being shot at with arrows. And many other biblical examples could be given. As weapons are used to destroy a person's body, evil words are used to destroy a person's soul. The Bible is very explicit about this. *Destructive words do violence to the soul.* Sometimes destructive words are referred to as verbal abuse, but I propose that this term does not even do it justice according to the biblical descriptions. According to the Bible, it's more like murder through words, or verbal assassination! This is serious stuff. And demonic assignments are released when we come under this type of verbal assault.

Just like words of encouragement, blessing, and prophecy can be inspired by the Holy Spirit and impart grace, destructive and corrupt words can be inspired by the devil. Even Peter, one of Jesus' main disciples, once spoke words that were influenced by satan (see Matthew 16:23). Words of accusation, unrighteous judgment, slander, and otherwise malicious words can release demonic assignments against the ones spoken to or spoken about. The Bible says that we are to take the shield of faith in order to protect us from the fiery darts of the wicked one (see Ephesians 6:16). I have found that one of the ways that the devil's flaming arrows come to us is through people's destructive and bitter words (see Psalm 64:2-4, quoted above).

Bitter words filled with anger or hatred are like arrows being shot at a person. False accusations and authoritative negative statements can release curses. There have been multiple occasions when I felt as though I were coming under unusual spiritual warfare, only to find out that there were false accusations, slander, and other malicious words being spoken about me behind closed doors. These words were releasing evil spirits and demonic assignments against me that needed to be resisted and broken off of me. Thankfully, we can stand on the promise of Isaiah 54:17:

> *"No weapon formed against you shall prosper,*
> *And every tongue which rises against you in judgment*
> *You shall condemn.*
> *This is the heritage of the servants of the Lord,*
> *And their righteousness is from Me,"*
> *Says the Lord.*

Breaking Word Curses

Anne came to the front of the church at the end of the service. As a guest speaker at a conference, I had taught on keys for getting free from evil spirits and led the whole congregation in a prayer for receiving deliverance. Anne told me that she would often have suicidal thoughts and feelings of self-hatred, especially when she was at church services. She also had trouble sleeping and would be tormented in her thoughts at night.

As I began to pray for Anne, I sensed the Holy Spirit prompting me to break the power of destructive words that had been spoken over her. When I did this, she crumpled to the floor and began to expel evil spirits from her mouth as I commanded them to leave. Once the prayer time was complete, she felt much relief and had peace in her mind. She testified the next morning that she had been delivered and had slept like a baby that night!

Like Anne's testimony, I have seen many cases of people being delivered from evil spirits when word curses and destructive words were broken from their life. If we want to break free from the power of destructive words, here are some steps we can pray through:

1. **Forgive the person:** Choose to forgive the person who spoke the words. This does not mean that we will automatically trust them or let them back into our lives, but we can release them to the Lord and choose to bless them. We must not allow anger, bitterness, or unforgiveness to have any place in our heart.

2. **Renounce the words:** Break the power of the words by renouncing them. You can say something like, "In the name of Jesus, I break the power of these words and cancel their power in my life. I command them to be uprooted from my soul." Be specific about the exact things that were spoken.

3. **Cast out the spirits:** Command every unclean spirit that is attached to these words to come out of you in the name of Jesus. Use the authority of Jesus' name to drive the evil spirits away and break every demonic assignment against you.

4. **Replace with truth and blessing:** Speak the opposite of what was spoken over you, and replace the curse with God's blessing. Speak the truth of God's Word over your life and ask Him to fill you afresh with the Holy Spirit. Let His love fill your heart and bring healing to your soul.

Yes, words can be destructive. But we do not need to live under the demonic oppression that the enemy is trying to release against us. There is deliverance in the name of Jesus. Call on His name and be set free from the influence of destructive words! You can use the following prayer to guide you in this process:

> *Heavenly Father, I ask for Your Holy Spirit to come and bring healing to me from any effects of word curses, slander, and false accusations. In Jesus' name, I forgive the ones who spoke destructive words into my life. I let go of any pain, bitterness, or resentment against them.*
>
> *I renounce the power of any curses or destructive words that have influence in my life. I uproot them from my soul in Jesus' name. I break the specific word curse that said _____.*
>
> *In the name of Jesus, I command any unclean spirits associated with word curses or malicious words to come out right now. I rebuke every lying spirit, spirit of slander, and spirit of accusation and command them to leave me in Jesus' name.*
>
> *Father God, I receive Your truth and blessing over my life. I receive a greater revelation of Your love for me and of my identity in Christ. In Jesus' name, amen!*

Ungodly Soul Ties

Another area that I want to address in this chapter is severing ungodly soul ties. God created us as relational beings. Healthy relationships are a building block of life and are necessary for our growth and development. However, when relationships are unhealthy, they have the potential to create bondages in our lives. Sometimes evil spirits can gain access to a person's life through unhealthy relationships and ungodly bonds.

The term *soul tie* is simply a reference to a deep bond with another person. This can be godly or ungodly, depending on the situation. David and Jonathan walked in a covenant friendship together, and the

Bible says that "the soul of Jonathan was knit to the soul of David" (1 Samuel 18:1). The marriage covenant, and sexual intimacy between a husband and wife, creates a bond where the "two become one" (see Genesis 2:24). These are examples of good and godly bonds. But there are other types of connections that are unhealthy and toxic, and these can be a doorway to demonic access. These ungodly soul ties seem to create an invisible bondage to the person involved.

One of the main ways that ungodly soul ties are created is through sexual intimacy outside of marriage. God created sex to bring oneness in marriage. Any sexual activity outside of the marriage covenant between a husband and wife is a violation of God's design and is therefore a perversion. Engaging in sexual relationships outside of marriage creates an ungodly bond, and this can give evil spirits an open door. Let's look at the apostle Paul's words in First Corinthians 6:15-20 (ESV):

> Do you not know that your bodies are members of Christ? Shall I then take the members of Christ and make them members of a prostitute? Never! Or do you not know that he who is joined to a prostitute becomes one body with her? For, as it is written, "The two will become one flesh." But he who is joined to the Lord becomes one spirit with him. Flee from sexual immorality. Every other sin a person commits is outside the body, but the sexually immoral person sins against his own body. Or do you not know that your body is a temple of the Holy Spirit within you, whom you have from God? You are not your own, for you were bought with a price. So glorify God in your body.

Paul clearly states that sexual intimacy creates a oneness with the person whom you engage with, whether or not the person is your spouse. When we give ourselves to someone sexually, a bond is created. Sex is a sacred act, reserved only for the marital relationship.

When this standard is violated, bonds are created with other people that were never meant to be created. These type of sexual soul ties can cause an attachment to someone and allow for demons to enter. (This gives a whole other meaning to STDs—it is not just sexually transmitted diseases that we should worry about, but also *sexually transmitted demons!*)

Other Examples of Ungodly Bonds

Another way that ungodly soul ties are created is when there is a destructive or toxic relationship with another individual. Examples include abuse of any kind, manipulation, control, and co-dependency. Relationships of this nature cause great damage and an unhealthy tie that needs to be broken.

When a person is in an abusive relationship, there is a bond that gets created. Counselors sometimes call this a *trauma bond*. God intends for us to bond with others in healthy ways: mutual love and respect, healthy communication, sharing of hearts, God-ordained friendships and connections, and other godly and loving ways. There is never meant to be control and domination of another person's will, or co-dependent attachments. We are meant to need each other in a healthy, interdependent way, but our main source of love and fulfillment is meant to come from our relationship with God.

In an abusive relationship, a bond is created on the basis of control, fear, and trauma. This bond sometimes keeps people attached to the ones who have abused them or keeps them in a cycle of abuse. Even when there is a physical separation from the abusive individual, there can be a spiritual connection that still remains. This can come from a one-time traumatic act, such as sexual abuse, or an ongoing pattern of abusive behavior. (The abuse in these situations might be sexual, verbal, spiritual, emotional, physical, or a combination of these.)

A final type of soul tie that I have come across is related to the occult. When a person gets involved in occult groups, there is often a leader whom you connect to, bond with, and give allegiance to. It is the devil's counterfeit of discipleship. The same principle can be applied to secret societies and spiritually abusive cults. Sometimes ties like this need to be severed when people are coming out of these types of destructive scenarios.

Prayer to Sever Ungodly Soul Ties

Thomas came as a visitor to the young adult service that my wife and I were leading several years ago. I was on staff at a church as a youth and young adult pastor and we had recently seen God begin to move in healing and deliverance in our Friday night young adult meetings. I felt the need to teach on deliverance to give some understanding of what was happening, and that night was my first message on the topic.

When I finished my message and gave an invitation for ministry, Thomas jetted to the front. He told me that he was coming out of an immoral relationship and needed deliverance and freedom from the tie to this woman. I anointed him with oil and barely began to pray when he suddenly fell backward to the ground. A demon began to manifest, his countenance turned angry, and he gripped the leg of a nearby chair as if he was about to throw it! Thankfully, God's peace was upon me and I knelt down next to him and calmly ministered to him until he was delivered. He later said that it was as if he was pinned to the floor and unable to move until the demon left. Praise God!

There is deliverance from ungodly bonds and destructive soul ties. Whether the bond was created through sexual sin, a toxic or abusive relationship, or some other way, we have authority to break free in the name of Jesus. Use the following prayer as a guide to sever every ungodly soul tie.

Heavenly Father, I thank You that You are a relational God and that You made us to have healthy and loving relationships. Help me to relate to You and others in the way that You intend and help me to discern when there is an unhealthy bond.

I repent of any sexual sin that I have committed and sever any ungodly soul ties that have been created. I set myself free from any unhealthy relationship or ungodly bond to another person. In the name of Jesus, I break the power of any bonds that have been created through abuse or trauma.

In particular, I break the tie with _____.
I declare that the blood of Jesus separates me from him/her. Now in the name of Jesus, I command any unclean spirits that have entered my life through ungodly soul ties or unhealthy bonds to come out. Go now, in Jesus' name!

| 12 |

SETTING OUR CHILDREN FREE

live in Lancaster County, Pennsylvania, which is known for its deep religious heritage in the Amish and Mennonite traditions. A few years ago, I was asked to teach on deliverance at a youth group for a Mennonite church that is over three hundred years old. There were about 25 high school students present that evening. As I began to share my message about demons and deliverance, it felt like I was up against a thick atmosphere of unbelief. This was a brand-new topic for these young people, and they seemed very closed to the idea. But about halfway through my message, something shifted.

I could see that some of the students were beginning to experience the beginning stages of demonic manifestations. So, I paused my message and said, "Right now, some of you are beginning to feel things shifting and moving in your body. Don't be alarmed. The demons are getting nervous because they are about to be expelled." As soon as I said this, several of the youth began to cry as they knew

I was speaking directly to them. The entire atmosphere changed, and everyone in the room was fixated on the message.

Once the message was complete, I led the group in a prayer for deliverance and began to cast out evil spirits. The once shy and closed-off group had changed dramatically. One young lady shook back and forth violently, as she was being delivered from demons that had come into her life through traumatic events she had experienced. Others trembled, others cried, and others quietly received freedom. In all, about half of the students were visibly set free from evil spirits that night.

This was a powerful reminder for me of how our young people are in need of deliverance. And keep in mind that this was not a group of at-risk street kids who were regularly exposed to crime and the drug culture. This was a group of students at a conservative Mennonite church. We must find a way to incorporate deliverance into the lives of the children and youth in our families and churches.

Children Who Are Captive

I have found that youth and children of all ages can need deliverance from demonic influence. This may seem surprising to some, but the Bible gives examples of children in need of deliverance. I believe that in many cases, some of the demonic influence that people wrestle with in adulthood had its origins in childhood. Below are two examples of children who needed deliverance in the New Testament.

1. **The Syro-Phoenician woman's daughter:** "For a woman whose young daughter had an unclean spirit heard about Him, and she came and fell at His feet. The woman was a Greek, a Syro-Phoenician by birth, and she kept asking Him to cast the demon out of her daughter" (Mark 7:25-26). Notice it describes the girl as the woman's *young daughter*. This was a child who was being harassed by a tormenting spirit. The mother persisted in faith and would not take

no for an answer. Jesus set the daughter free through a pronouncement that the demon had gone out of her, even though she was not present.

2. A young boy: In Mark 9:14-29, there was a boy with a mute spirit who was being tormented and oppressed. Jesus asked the boy's father how long he had been in this condition and the father replied, "From childhood" (Mark 9:21). Jesus commanded the evil spirit to come out of the boy and he was delivered.

These stories show us the reality that children can need deliverance from evil spirits. And I suspect that this is more common than we realize. How do children end up under demonic influence and in need of deliverance? Just like with adults, there are various factors and each situation is unique. It could be through trauma or abuse that they have endured at a young age or dark things that they were exposed to. It could be through generational curses passed through the family line. It could be through occultic influences in the home. As they get older, it could be through their own rebellion and sin.

What Our Young People Are Facing

Several years ago, I went on a youth retreat as a volunteer leader. On one of the nights, the guest speaker gave a message on the baptism of the Holy Spirit and invited students to come forward to be empowered by the Spirit. Several were being touched by God and filled with the Holy Spirit at the altar, but one particular seventh grader named Ashley caught my attention. When the speaker laid hands on her, she fell to the ground. As she lay there, I could tell that she was not simply being touched by the Lord, but that something else was going on. She began to cry in a way that showed she was upset or disturbed about something, and her facial expression was not one of peace but of anguish.

After a few minutes, I began to suspect that Ashley was being tormented by a demon. But since I was not in charge of the meeting,

I hesitated to take any action. After a while, she went back to her seat. She continued to cry in a tormented way as her friends tried to console her. Finally, I decided to go and pray for her. I sat next to her and felt prompted to anoint her head with a dab of anointing oil. But when I reached to put the oil on her forehead, she abruptly threw her head to the side to avoid being anointed. Now I knew that an evil spirit was at work and was resisting being expelled. I moved her away from her friends to a more private area, asked the youth pastor and his wife to join me, and ministered to her. I commanded the evil spirit to leave her and within a few minutes it left, exiting through her mouth.

Ashley's countenance returned to normal and she rejoiced in her freedom. I later found out that there was trauma and strife in her family, and this was what had opened the door to the demonic influence she had experienced.

Our young people are up against so much in today's society. Broken homes, abuse, and family trauma. Entertainment that is filled with violence, sexual immorality, magic, and dark paranormal activity. Pressure to be sexually active and increasing exposure to pornography. Social media comparison and constant peer pressure to fit in. Access to drugs and alcohol, and the culture of partying. These are just some of the issues facing and pulling at our young people.

The devil is clearly after our children. Just the other day I was in a local bookstore and was shocked to see books on yoga, meditation, and astrology that were aimed at *babies*. This is not a time to play games in the Church and ignore or merely entertain our youth and children. This is a time to do battle for a generation to experience true freedom, encounter the living God, and live in consecration to Jesus. This should stir the hearts of church leaders and parents alike to contend for revival among our young people.

Spiritual Warfare for Our Children

Christian parents must realize the critical role that they play in their children's spiritual growth and spiritual protection. Too often, parents outsource the spiritual development of their children to their local church. I fully believe in having strong youth and children's ministries. But these are to be a supplement to what is happening at home. It is the role of Christian parents to teach, train, and discipline their children in the ways of the Lord. This must all be done in the context of a healthy and loving relationship with them. Parents should lead by example, build a genuine connection with their children, and commit to raise them in the Lord as best as they know how. None of us will do this perfectly, and we trust God to make up where we have lacked. But we cannot shirk our responsibility in training our children.

We should be very careful with what we allow into our homes and what entertainment we allow our children to partake in. We should be diligent to consistently intercede for our children. And we should ask the Holy Spirit for wisdom in navigating times of spiritual attack on our children. If all of this sounds like a full-time job, it's because it is! Parenting is a major calling and responsibility that we carry, meant to take time, energy, and focus.

I have seen firsthand the need to be vigilant when it comes to the spiritual battle for our children. When our son was seven years old, my wife and I noticed a time when he began to act out in strange ways. More than normal sibling squabbles, he was attacking his younger sister in ways that were sinister and out of character. This went on for a few days and culminated when we had to come home early from a date because our babysitter reached out for help. Our son has times of difficulty like any other child, but is generally pretty kind and obedient. This behavior was highly unusual!

That night, my wife and I spent some time praying together for our son before going to sleep. We were asking for specific insight and strategy for what to do. I sensed that the Holy Spirit was prompting me to go into my son's room while he was asleep, anoint him with oil, and pray to break off any assignments of the enemy. I obeyed this prompting and my son slept right through it. The whole thing only took a minute or two and was very simple. But the next morning, there was a marked difference, and his behavior returned to normal. Something had lifted off in the prayer time the night before.

Another time when a demonic spirit tried to attach itself to my young son was during a time of great grief for our family. My wife's brother was tragically killed in a car accident, and this sudden death was a shock to all of us. Our son was quite impacted by this, as he loved his uncle. As a young seven-year-old, he was faced with the reality of tragedy and death for the first time. He wrestled through questions about the goodness of God and how this could happen. And he was also beginning to develop a fear of death. Especially at night, he would be troubled by thoughts of losing a parent or never seeing one of us again.

Within a month of this time, we were in worship during a Sunday morning church service. I felt a strong impression from the Holy Spirit that there was an anointing for deliverance and that I should pray to break off the spirit of death and the spirit of suicide. I didn't take a lot of time, but I went up and took the microphone and began to pray over the congregation, not thinking at all about my son. As I rebuked the spirit of death, my young son began to have a mild manifestation—he yawned a wide, uncontrollable yawn and began to feel as though he would throw up. I didn't exactly realize what was going on, but my wife moved him to a separate area and prayed over him until the spirit left. He was no longer troubled with the fear of death after that time of prayer. Praise God for how the Holy Spirit led and intervened!

While my son's situations mentioned above may not have been overly severe, they were real spiritual battles. What would have happened if we had not been in tune with the Holy Spirit and the spiritual dynamics that were at work? Could things have gotten worse? I believe so. While we shouldn't be overzealous about deliverance and spiritual warfare with our children, we should be aware and ready to minister to them when needed. Let's not neglect basic discipline and training, blaming everything on the devil. But let's also not neglect spiritual realities that are at work.

Ministering Deliverance to Children

Jesus had a value for children and loved to minister to them, breaking the cultural norms of His day. Below is one such example.

> *Then children were brought to him that he might lay his hands on them and pray. The disciples rebuked the people, but Jesus said, "Let the little children come to me and do not hinder them, for to such belongs the kingdom of heaven." And he laid his hands on them and went away* (Matthew 19:13-15 ESV).

Even today, we can easily belittle and look down on our children, not taking them seriously and believing they don't have much to offer spiritually. But this is a grave mistake. Kids can know God at a young age, be empowered by the Holy Spirit, hear God's voice, and minister to others. They can have a real relationship with God. My wife and I have personally seen this reality in our own children, and we have seen it with the children in our church as well.

A few years ago, God strongly highlighted the kids in our local church. We revamped our kids ministry, wrote our own twelve-month kid's curriculum (called *Kids Empowered*), and became much more intentional with receiving our children as vital members of our church family. It has been awesome to see God at work in our children!

Several Sundays a year, I will go back into our kids ministry area and speak for a special kids service with our children in kindergarten through sixth grade. One of those times, we had an emphasis on deliverance. After a time of worship, I taught a basic message on deliverance from evil spirits. I used object lessons that would help engage the kids, and was sure to teach in a way that was understandable and not scary. After the message, I led the children in a time of receiving deliverance, and several of them were set free from demonic influence.

Our teenagers and children are in need of ministry, just as adults are. Jesus referred to deliverance as "the children's bread" before He eventually delivered the Syro-Phoenician woman's young daughter from demonic torment (see Mark 7:27). This is a symbolic reference to deliverance being the portion of the children of God, but we can also apply it to literal children. Deliverance belongs to the people of God, old and young. Let's not deprive our youth and children of any type of ministry, including deliverance. As Jesus embraced, empowered, and ministered to children, we should do the same.

When it comes to ministering deliverance to youth and children, here are some basic principles and guidelines that you will hopefully find helpful:

- In the biblical examples of deliverance for children, a parent was involved in bringing the child's need to Jesus. This is a good illustration of how parental engagement is an important part of a child receiving ministry. There can be exceptions to this when it may not be possible (for example, when parents are unbelievers). But the general rule is that it is best to have parental involvement. The parents themselves can be the best ones to minister to their children, but parents do not always feel equipped to minister deliverance.

- The older the child, the more involved they can and should be in the deliverance process. Teens can be engaged in the same way that adults can, and they are old enough to understand the concepts of salvation and exercise their will to close doors and resist the devil. Many pre-teens can also be engaged in the process as well.

- Young children, toddlers, and infants can be prayed over while they are asleep. They do not necessarily need to be involved in the prayer time, and oftentimes might be too young to engage or fully understand what is happening.

- When explaining the concept of deliverance to young children, make sure to use language and a tone of voice that does not cause fear. Use words and terms that are understandable (for example, you can call demons "bad spirits"). Always emphasize the victory and power of Jesus over the devil and his demonic kingdom.

Maybe you're a parent of young children and teens. Maybe you're a children's pastor or kids ministry volunteer. Maybe you're a Sunday school teacher or teacher at a public or private school. Maybe you're a youth pastor or you volunteer with a ministry to teens. Whatever setting you may be in, be aware that children are in a very real spiritual battle. The devil doesn't wait until children are grown up to begin his assault on them. Neither should we wait to lead them to Jesus, minister to them, and set them free from powers of darkness.

Arming Our Children with Spiritual Weapons

We can minister to our children and see them encounter God and walk in freedom. Some children need to be set free from captivity just as adults do. Jesus came for them too, and He demonstrated His heart for them in His earthly ministry. How much better for a child to receive deliverance at a young age than to wait so many years and only find freedom later in life?

We can begin to teach our children about the reality of satan and the kingdom of darkness. As we do this, we must never do so in a way that conjures fear of the devil. Jesus is so much greater than the devil. He has defeated him through His work on the cross and has paid the price for our salvation and deliverance. So, as we teach our kids about spiritual warfare, we should do it with Christ's victory and God's greatness as the backdrop. But we must not shy away from telling our kids about these realities, thinking that they are too young or that it will only scare them.

Children need to know how to use spiritual weapons to overcome the evil one. They should learn how to pray and declare God's Word when they face temptation or spiritual attack. They should learn about the power of the blood of Jesus and how praise is a weapon in our spiritual warfare. They should learn how to resist the devil so that he will flee.

Let's not hold back in teaching our children spiritual realities. Let's engage them at their level and teach them the truths of God's Word in a way that they can understand and apply to their lives. Let's equip them for the battle that they are in and give them the tools they need to overcome the evil one!

| 13 |

ESTABLISHED IN FREEDOM

A s we have seen throughout this book, our God is the God who heals, restores, and sets captives free. Let's look once again at our theme passage from Isaiah 61, this time reading further than verse 1.

> *The Spirit of the Lord God is upon Me,*
> *Because the Lord has anointed Me*
> *To preach good tidings to the poor;*
> *He has sent Me to heal the brokenhearted,*
> *To proclaim liberty to the captives,*
> *And the opening of the prison to those who are bound;*
> *To proclaim the acceptable year of the Lord,*
> *And the day of vengeance of our God;*
> *To comfort all who mourn,*
> *To console those who mourn in Zion,*

To give them beauty for ashes,

The oil of joy for mourning,

The garment of praise for the spirit of heaviness;

That they may be called trees of righteousness,

The planting of the Lord, that He may be glorified.

And they shall rebuild the old ruins,

They shall raise up the former desolations,

And they shall repair the ruined cities,

The desolations of many generations (Isaiah 61:1-4).

I love the progression of this passage. The first phase emphasizes restoration, healing, and deliverance to those in need. And God does not simply remove the ashes, He replaces them with beauty. He doesn't just take away mourning, He fills us with the oil of joy. He not only lifts off the spirit of heaviness, He also replaces it with a garment of praise. And He is not content for us to only be delivered, He wants us to be planted as "trees of righteousness." He wants us to be established and rooted in our freedom.

Then, to take it a step further, the very ones who were set free and established become the ones who reach out to others to set them free—rebuilding the old ruins and repairing the desolated cities. This is how God redeems. You get free, stay free, and then you get to set others free!

Established in Freedom

It is important to understand that deliverance is not meant to be an end in itself. It is a means to propel us forward in our relationship with God and the purposes that He has for our lives. Once the chains and fetters are removed, we can step into more of all that the Lord intends for us. We can love Him and others better now that we have experienced His love in this way. We can serve better, now that we are free in our emotions and minds. We can reach others, now that we are no longer bound. As important as it is to break free from the chains of demonic influence, it is just as important that we stay free and move into God's purposes.

Jesus indicated that when an evil spirit leaves a person it may attempt to reenter and even bring some friends along.

> *When an unclean spirit goes out of a man, he goes through dry places, seeking rest, and finds none. Then he says, "I will return to my house from which I came." And when he comes, he finds it empty, swept, and put in order. Then he goes and takes with him seven other spirits more wicked than himself, and they enter and dwell there; and the last state of that man is worse than the first...* (Matthew 12:43-45).

This passage should not make us afraid, but aware that we must be vigilant to resist the devil. He is a defeated foe and no match for Jesus, but that does not mean that we can be lackadaisical in our approach to spiritual warfare. When a person is set free from evil spirits, it is important that they close every door that allowed the spirits to be there in the first place. But it is also important to fill the "house" with the attributes of Christ. In the above passage, the returning spirit finds the house empty. We do not just want a house that is empty— free of evil spirits—we want a house that is filled with the nature and presence of God. We want to be filled with the Word of God and with the Holy Spirit. A person who is filled with the love, truth, and light of God, and has closed the door to the enemy, will repel evil spirits.

Those who are delivered from demons should be aware that the demons may seek to regain entrance. But there is a big difference between fighting off evil spirits from the outside and having the pressure, temptation, or torment from the inside. A person who has been delivered will find that they can much more readily choose freedom.

What used to feel like a compulsive and enslaving pressure toward sin is now an outward temptation that can be resisted. What used to feel like hopeless torment and oppression is now a momentary battle that can be won in Christ. What used to seem like something that was intertwined with a person's identity has now been removed so that freedom can reign.

I have noticed a pattern that after deliverance, a spirit may come back and seek to reenter once or twice, but if successfully resisted it will eventually stop coming around. It recognizes that it will not be able to regain entrance and tries to find another "house" to dwell in. While the above passage of Scripture should not make us scared to get delivered, it should cause us to realize that we must be serious about getting free and staying free. We must be on guard against the attack of the enemy and be prepared to resist him.

Renewing the Mind

One of the keys for being established in freedom is the renewal of the mind. When a person is delivered from demonic chains, it is important that old and faulty mindsets are replaced with the truth. Some people are accustomed to walking in bondage and torment and have believed the enemy's lies for many years. They may have thought patterns that are contrary to the truth of God's Word, and must learn to recognize these patterns so that their minds can be renewed with truth. Romans 12:2 says that we are to be transformed by the renewing of our minds. If we do not have our minds renewed, we can fall into old habits and become vulnerable to the devil's attempt to reenter our lives. But if we will allow our minds to be renewed, not only will we walk in freedom, but we will be truly transformed.

The mind is a primary target of spiritual battle, and we must not allow evil spirits to have any access in this area. If we are to walk in the fullness of freedom, not only must we allow the Holy Spirit to renew our mind, we must also learn how to take our thoughts captive.

For the weapons of our warfare are not carnal but mighty in God for pulling down strongholds, casting down arguments and every high thing that exalts itself against the knowledge of God, bringing every thought into captivity to the obedience of Christ (2 Corinthians 10:4-5).

Did you know that you do not have to be subject to every thought that comes into your mind? Not every thought that you have is from you. The enemy is constantly assaulting us and planting thoughts in our mind. We can't always control the thoughts that enter, but we can control what we do with them. Learn to take charge of your thoughts instead of passively allowing whatever thought that comes in to remain and continue to have influence. If a thought enters your mind that is contrary to God, take it captive and push it out. Practically speaking, this can be as simple as praying a quick prayer or making a scriptural declaration that denies the thought.

One of the practices that can help in the process of renewing your mind is to make biblical declarations. You do this by taking a particular Scripture verse, personalizing it, and proclaiming it out loud. For example, if you have been delivered from fear and are walking out that freedom, you can make a declaration based on Second Timothy 1:7: *God has not given me a spirit of fear, but of power and of love and of a sound mind.* Or you can proclaim the truth found in 1 John 4:18, applying it to yourself: *God's perfect love has cast all fear out of my life.* God's Word is powerful, and we are built up in faith when we hear it and declare it over ourselves. Find Bible verses that are relevant to your situation and use the "sword of the Spirit" to stand against the devil and his demons. (See Appendix 4 for examples of biblical declarations.)

Principles for Staying Free

A passage that I often share with people in relation to deliverance is James 4:7-8: "Therefore submit to God. Resist the devil and he will flee from you. Draw near to God and He will draw near to you." Within this short passage there is one unconditional command and two conditional promises. Let's break down this passage in more detail, keeping in mind that these principles will help us to be established in our freedom once we have been set free from demonic influence.

1. Submit to God

Submission to God is not an optional suggestion for believers to take into consideration. It is the command of God to us, and we should take it seriously. This means that we must yield every area of our lives to the lordship of Jesus. We can no longer be our own masters, for we have been bought at a price. Many want Jesus to be their Savior, but how many want Him to be their Lord? Submission to Jesus as Lord is exemplified in our obedience to Him—obedience to the written Word and obedience to the direction of the Holy Spirit. Jesus once asked an interesting and challenging question: "Why do you call Me 'Lord, Lord,' and not do the things which I say?" (Luke 6:46). In other words, *Why do you call Me the boss but act like you are the boss? Why do you give lip service to My lordship but not follow through with obedience?*

We cannot afford to live in a double lifestyle, half-hearted devotion, or agreement with sin. We cannot simply go to church on Sunday morning to check it off the list, but live like God does not exist the rest of the week. Jesus is looking for true disciples. This means submitting to Him as Lord of your life.

Submitting to God means being quick to acknowledge and repent of sin if we stumble. It means that we agree with His Word and follow His ways. Living a lifestyle of submission to God will be a safeguard against the assault of the enemy and will help us to continue to walk in the freedom we have received.

2. Resist the Devil

From the posture of being in submission to God, the next part of the James 4 passage quoted above gives a conditional promise: if we resist the devil, then he will flee from us. It is important to see that even though satan is ultimately defeated, we must actively resist him in order to live in victory over him. Consider also the charge given to us in First Peter 5:8-9: "Be sober, be vigilant; because your adversary the devil walks about like a roaring lion, seeking whom he may devour. Resist him, steadfast in the faith, knowing that the same sufferings are experienced by your brotherhood in the world." The enemy of our souls is seeking to devour us, and we must be steadfast to stand against him.

When a person is delivered from evil spirits, it should not come as a surprise that the enemy may try to counterattack. In fact, as we have already seen, the Bible indicates that evil spirits seek to reenter the very people from whom they have been evicted. With that being the case, it is important for the person who has been delivered to be prepared to resist the attack of the devil. We are told that we are in a spiritual battle and must wear spiritual armor (see Ephesians 6:10-18). We are to be alert and vigilant to stand against the kingdom of darkness.

The word *resist* in both James 4:7 and First Peter 5:9 is the same Greek word. It is an active word that means to set yourself against, withstand, or oppose. We are to set ourselves against the devil. We must not make any agreement with him or his ways. We must absolutely make him and his demons our enemies and not entertain them in any way. Just as Jesus did, we can use the Word of God to stand against the devil.

3. Draw Near to God

James goes on to say, "Draw near to God and He will draw near to you" (James 4:8). This is truly an exciting promise; God Himself will draw near to us as we draw near to Him. God is personal and He desires a relationship with His children. As we draw near to Him in worship, prayer, Bible study, fellowship with other believers, and through other spiritual practices, He will reveal Himself to us and become more real in our lives. Drawing near may take discipline and will certainly take time; but the reward is God Himself. There is no greater reward than knowing Him.

While deliverance from demons is wonderful, it should not be seen as an end in itself. It is a means to growing in intimacy with the Lord and walking in the fullness of our destiny. Intimacy with God should be our highest goal. Everything else we do in our Christian walk flows out of a lifestyle of relationship with God. And as we draw near to the Lord and grow in our relationship with Him, a natural by-product will be that it will help us continue in the freedom we have received. As we are filled with His Word, as we hear His voice, as we allow His presence to permeate our lives, His light will repel the darkness.

When a person is delivered from demons, if they will focus on these areas—submitting to God, resisting the devil, and drawing near to the Lord—they will not need to worry constantly about maintaining their freedom. It will happen in the process of their spiritual growth and walk with the Lord. So, while we must be aware of the enemy's counterattack and the need to stay free, we don't need to waste unnecessary energy being worried that we will fall back into bondage or oppression.

Be transformed by the renewing of your mind. Learn to take thoughts captive. Submit to God. Resist the devil. Draw near to God. These are the keys for staying free!

Deliverance Is Not a Cure-All

One more thing I want to emphasize before the close of this chapter is that deliverance is not a cure-all. When you first learn about deliverance, it is easy to think that you now have the answer to every problem that you may face. And while many issues are caused by demonic influence, the truth is that deliverance is not a cure-all. As powerful and necessary as this ministry is, it is not the solution to every problem, and it will not make all of your problems go away. Jesus said that we would have trouble in this world, and Paul said that we enter the Kingdom through many tribulations (see John 16:33 and Acts 14:22). Don't think that being delivered from demons will make all of your problems disappear.

It is also important to remember that we have three enemies: the world system, the flesh, and the devil. Not every negative issue is caused by a demon; many times, we are dealing with the flesh and need to act accordingly. This is one of the reasons why cultivating discernment is important. If a problem is caused by a demon, we need deliverance. If it is an issue of the flesh, we need to overcome by walking in the Spirit and exercising self-control. We crucify the flesh, but you can't crucify a demon; it must be cast out.

Deliverance should also not be seen as a replacement for other areas of our Christian journey. When a person receives freedom from demonic influence it can cause them to begin to grow rapidly in the Lord. Chains that held them back are no longer there, and they can move forward in their walk with God, gifts, and calling. Deliverance, however, is not a substitute for spiritual disciplines such as prayer, fasting, time in the Word, and fellowship with other believers in a local church. In other words, deliverance should not be seen as a shortcut. You will still need to exercise discipline, learn to resist the enemy, and walk in the Spirit on a daily basis.

When evil spirits are present in a person's life, there is no substitute for the ministry of deliverance. Counseling can be necessary and important for various types of situations. But remember that you can't counsel away a demon. Nor can you exercise enough discipline for demons to go away. Again, evil spirits must be cast out. At the same time, let's be careful not to make deliverance a substitute for other important practices. There is no substitute for time spent in the presence of God and for meditating on God's Word regularly. There is no substitute for discipleship and good teaching. There is no substitute for connection to fellow believers in the local church. None of these take the place of the others; they all have an important place in our walk with God.

We must fully embrace the ministry of deliverance. It is much needed today and so many captives are waiting to be set free. But let's also remember to keep the ministry of deliverance in its proper place. Deliverance is not the whole; it is a part. And while it is a very significant part, it can become error when it is isolated from the rest of biblical truth and practice. We want to see deliverance restored to the Church in a healthy way and we want to keep our focus on Jesus in the process.

As we close this chapter, be encouraged that God wants to set you free, establish you in freedom, and then empower you to bring deliverance to others. In fact, I believe that God is raising up a mighty army to set the captives free!

| 14 |

RAISING UP AN ARMY TO SET CAPTIVES FREE

illiam came as a visitor to Threshold Church where I serve as lead pastor. He was reluctant to visit because he was a little uneasy about Charismatic churches and the gifts of the Holy Spirit. He was in town from out of state for a short while before heading back home, and one of his good friends had invited him to church. He made a last-minute decision to come. Little did he know that we were having a deliverance service that morning.

During the ministry time, I led the congregation through a prayer of deliverance and then began to minister corporately. As I was commanding evil spirits to come out of people, William was set free from unclean spirits related to lust and sexual sin. No one laid hands on him or prayed for him personally, and yet he was powerfully delivered. But it didn't stop there. When William got back home, he connected with a group of believers who began to minister deliverance to others. He went from being skeptical of supernatural ministry, to getting set free from bondage, to being used to set others free. This is an example of how the ministry of deliverance can be multiplied!

Jesus Multiplied the Ministry of Deliverance

Throughout this book, I have emphasized that Jesus came to set captives free. It was a part of His commission and one of the reasons why the Holy Spirit came upon Him. But Jesus was not the only One who freed people from evil spirits. When He called the twelve disciples to follow Him, He specifically equipped them to minister deliverance: "Then He appointed twelve, that they might be with Him and that He might send them out to preach, and to have power to heal sicknesses and to cast out demons" (Mark 3:14-15). Notice that they were to do the same things that Jesus did, including casting out demons. This was a normal part of following Jesus.

We see this play out as the Gospels unfold. After a period of following Jesus for a time, He sent out the twelve and they cast out many demons:

> *And he called the twelve and began to send them out two by two, and gave them authority over the unclean spirits. ...So they went out and proclaimed that people should repent. And they cast out many demons and anointed with oil many who were sick and healed them* (Mark 6:7,12-13 ESV).

Expanding the ministry further, Jesus sent out 70 others also, who came back from their "mission trip" rejoicing that evil spirits were subject to them (see Luke 10:17). Finally, He gave the commission to cast out demons to the whole Church: "And these signs will follow those who believe: In My name they will cast out demons..." (Mark 16:17).

Notice that Jesus was continually expanding the ministry of deliverance. He was not trying to be an exclusive exorcist who alone could free people from demonic influence. He intentionally multiplied this ministry so that more and more people could be set free. And I believe that He is doing the same thing in our day.

Making Deliverance Normal Again

While God is highlighting the ministry of deliverance in this hour and moving sovereignly to raise up ministers, there is a responsibility to cooperate with Him in this process. If we want to equip and release an army of deliverers and see more captives set free, there are some intentional things that we can do. The first step to multiplying the ministry of deliverance is to make it a normal part of the culture of the Church again. It was normal for Jesus and His followers, and it should be normal for us as well.

Some people are concerned that if we start to talk about demons and deliverance, we will become too fixated and excessively focused on it. While there may be some validity to these concerns, I am much more concerned with the significant percentage of churches that do not believe in or practice the ministry of deliverance at all. If deliverance from evil spirits was not meant to be a normal part of the Church's life and mission, then Jesus sure missed that memo!

Instead of taking our cues from our culture and church tradition, we must take our cues from Jesus. We must make deliverance a normal ministry that is incorporated into the life of the church. For the last few years, we have been working on cultivating this in our local church environment. Here are some practical things I have found helpful in making deliverance normal again.

1. Deliverance should be talked about and taught on openly: We should not avoid talking about or teaching this topic. Making deliverance a taboo subject only serves to perpetuate the fear, confusion, and stigma that is often attached to it. Biblical teaching that brings clarity to the reality of evil spirits and how to get free from them is a must. We must not be afraid of sounding foolish to some who will not embrace a supernatural worldview or concerned that we might offend some people. We must be more concerned with obeying Jesus, setting captives free, and equipping the saints for the work of ministry.

Deliverance can be taught from the pulpit, in home groups, Sunday school classes, seminars, and other settings. The point is not to obsess over the topic, but to bring it into the light and include it as a part of the overall spiritual diet of the Church.

2. Deliverance should be ministered publicly in a healthy way: Not only should deliverance be taught publicly, it is my belief that it should be ministered publicly as well. Every local church and ministry will have to determine their own protocol, of course, and there can be great value in deliverance being done in private prayer ministry settings. But in my opinion, we should not relegate deliverance ministry to private settings only.

Jesus did not avoid ministering deliverance in public, and I see no reason why we should either. We must do this in a healthy way, with compassion for the ones being ministered to, but we should not avoid public deliverance altogether. When we teach and minister deliverance openly, it demystifies the subject and opens the way for many others to be set free. I can't tell you how many people have been set free in public services. And people are often pleasantly surprised at the atmosphere of God's peace in the room, even when there are demonic manifestations.

3. Deliverance should be done along with pastoral care and discipleship: Deliverance and discipleship go hand in hand. When possible, we should follow up with those who receive ministry and make sure to have a way for them to be cared for and discipled. This is why the local church is the ideal setting for deliverance to happen. We have tended to outsource ministries like inner healing and deliverance to outside ministries, but I believe it will be even more effective when done in the context of the local church.

For some people, deliverance will be a process and a journey to wholeness and freedom. Including it as part of pastoral care and discipleship is a great way to have a more holistic approach, instead of being an isolated ministry.

4. We should include testimonies of deliverance: Again, we should not be ashamed to talk openly about deliverance. There are often testimonies in churches about healing, salvation, and God's provision. But it is rarer to have people sharing their testimony of deliverance. We have found it to be very powerful and effective when former captives share their story of freedom.

We should encourage people to share testimonies of their experience with deliverance when they are ready and willing. As deliverance is embraced as a part of the culture of a church or ministry, it becomes a normal thing to talk about. This helps to remove the unnecessary stigma and shame that is often associated with it and opens the door for others to be set free.

5. We should equip the average believer to minister deliverance: Jesus never set out to be an exclusive exorcist or intended for deliverance to be done only by an elite few. He intentionally multiplied the ministry of deliverance so that more people could be set free. We should do the same, equipping the average believer to be able to cast out evil spirits. Like any other area of ministry, some people will be more drawn to deliverance than others, and some will have more gifting in it. It is not that everyone should make it a primary focus, but every believer should know the basics of how to get free and set others free.

Effective equipping normally happens in multiple ways. Jesus taught, demonstrated, discipled, imparted, and sent His disciples. We can do the same, taking a multifaceted approach. I will often invite those I am equipping to be part of the ministry team when I minister at a deliverance meeting, or to join me when I am praying over someone in a private prayer ministry setting. Leaders should find practical ways to get more people involved through a healthy equipping process.

Are You Part of the Army?

When it comes to the need for deliverance, it is clear that this is an area where the harvest is plentiful, but the laborers are few (see Matthew 9:37). As we make deliverance a normal part of the culture of the Church, we can begin to raise up an army to set captives free. This will take time and intentionality; it will not happen overnight or without hard work and purposeful steps. But one day at a time, we can equip, empower, and release others to work in this ministry.

Perhaps you are feeling a stirring in your heart to be involved in casting out demons and setting captives free. How can you begin to get involved? Here are some steps you can take:

- **Seek God's heart:** Prioritize your relationship with God above all else, knowing that all true ministry will flow out of intimacy with Him. Cultivate God's heart of compassion for people so that you can have the right motives and minister in a place of God's love.

- **Learn as much as you can:** Study the Scriptures, read good books, attend seminars, and glean from trusted resources. This will help equip you and prepare you for what you will encounter when you cast out demons.

- **Connect with like-minded believers**: Find a local church or ministry that you can plug into, learn from, and step out in ministry. This can provide a safe covering for you to learn and grow. If you cannot find a place like this where you are located, look for one to connect with online as a supplement to your spiritual growth.

- **Ask for the Holy Spirit's power**: Live a lifestyle of prayer and fasting, and continually seek for a greater anointing of the Holy Spirit so that you can minister effectively. Ask the Lord to release His supernatural gifts in and through you to help set captives free.

- **Step out**: When you have opportunities, step out and minister. You don't have to have it all figured out to begin to minister deliverance. In my first experience with deliverance, I knew very little about what I was doing and had only had some equipping from a book I had read. But God moved, and demons were cast out. Use wisdom, but step out with boldness and confidence in your authority in Christ.

God is raising up an army to heal broken hearts, cast out demons, and set captives free. He is taking the ones who were once captive, establishing them in freedom, and sending them to bring deliverance to others. As more of this army steps into place, demons will tremble, chains will break, and destinies will be released. Will you be a part of this army?

Closing Prayer

As we come to the close of this book, let me pray over you as you continue to walk in freedom and set captives free:

Heavenly Father, I thank You for the person reading this book right now. Thank You for Your love for them and how You have paid the price for their salvation and deliverance through the death and resurrection of Your Son. I pray Your blessing and protection over them, and that You would guide them into all truth by Your Holy Spirit.

Continue to lead the one reading this book into greater places of freedom, holiness, and intimacy with You. Reveal Yourself to them, draw them closer to You, and allow them to know You more.

Father, I ask for the power of the Holy Spirit to come upon this person. Fill them with Your love and compassion, and give them a heart to see others walking in wholeness and freedom. I ask that You would equip them and anoint them to cast out demons and set captives free. In Jesus' precious name, amen!

OPEN DOORS TO DEMONIC INFLUENCE

The following is a list of common demonic access points. You can use this as a quick reference for yourself or when ministering to others.

This is not meant to be an exhaustive list, but it covers some of the most common open doors. In most cases where deliverance is needed, it is likely that one or more of these doors have been opened. Remember that each case will be unique, and that the guidance and discernment of the Holy Spirit is always needed.

1. Embracing Sin

- When we justify and embrace sin, we come into agreement with the devil and give him a place in our lives (see Ephesians 4:26-27).

- Premeditated sinful acts can open the door (e.g., adultery, deceiving, stealing, abortion).

2. Traumatic Experiences

- Being sinned against—especially when we are young—can open the door (e.g., abuse, abandonment, rejection).
- Other traumatic experiences can open the door (e.g., accidents, relational breakdowns, fearful events, violent crimes).
- Abusive events or ongoing abusive relationships (physical, sexual, emotional, verbal, spiritual).

3. Believing the Enemy's Lies

- A revelation of truth sets us free (see John 8:32); believing a lie brings bondage. When we believe a lie (about God, about ourselves, etc.) we come into agreement with the devil who is the "father of lies" (see John 8:44).

4. Exposure to Unholy Things

- Being exposed to unholy things can open the door (e.g., pornography, horror movies, dark music).

5. Unforgiveness

- Unforgiveness gives the devil God-given permission to torment and afflict us (see Matthew 18:21-35).

6. Involvement in False Religions, Cults, and False Teaching

- Behind every idol is a demon (see 1 Corinthians 10:19-20).

- False teaching carries with it a demonic spirit (see 2 Corinthians 11:4; 1 Timothy 4:1).

7. Any Occult Involvement

- Occult: hidden or secret arts. Supernatural knowledge or power through the demonic realm.
- Contact with the occult is a major open door to the demonic and is strictly forbidden in Scripture (see Deuteronomy 18:9-12).

8. Curses

- Generational curses: sinful and/or harmful patterns that pass through the family line (see Exodus 20:4-6)—e.g., alcoholism, abuse, suicide.
- Word curses: destructive and negative words spoken against us, especially when coming from authority figures (see James 3:8-10); slander and false accusations.
- Occult curses: curses/spells placed by those in the occult.

9. Ungodly Relationships/Soul Ties

- Spiritual/soulish/fleshly bonds created through ungodly sexual relationships (see 1 Corinthians 6:16).
- Unhealthy relationships that involve control, manipulation, intimidation, or abuse.

WHAT IS THE OCCULT?

The word *occult* means secret or hidden. It refers to tapping into the spiritual realm outside of the one true living God. The occult has a variety of branches and is far-reaching in influence. Scripture strictly forbids any contact with the occult, and such contact opens the door to evil spirits. Deuteronomy 18:9-12 is a passage that outlines various types of activities that fall into this category:

> *When you come into the land which the Lord your God is giving you, you shall not learn to follow the abominations of those nations. There shall not be found among you anyone who makes his son or his daughter pass through the fire, or one who practices witchcraft, or a soothsayer, or one who interprets omens, or a sorcerer, or one who conjures spells, or a medium, or a spiritist, or one who calls up the dead. For all who do these things are an abomination to the Lord, and*

because of these abominations the Lord your God drives them out from before you.

Below is a list of some of the most common branches of the occult, with some explanation and a few descriptions in each category. The list is not comprehensive, but covers many of the most basic forms of occult activity. There is a lot of overlap between many of these, and different people may practice them in different ways—the idea here is to give a brief overview. Involvement in these types of activities can range from curiosity and minor personal involvement to full-blown engagement with occult groups, covens, and secret societies:

- **Witchcraft:** The essence of witchcraft is to seek to control circumstances and people through spiritual power. The spirit of witchcraft works in a subtle way through manipulation, intimidation, guilt, and domination. When people move into the overt practice of witchcraft, they use rituals, curses, and other methods to influence people and circumstances. Related to witchcraft are wicca, satanism, voodoo, paganism, shamanism, santería, and similar activities.

- **Divination:** Divination is specifically related to seeking to tell the future or gain secret information through spiritual means. There are a variety of ways that this happens, including psychic powers, palm reading, tarot cards, fortunetelling, astrology, horoscopes, Ouija boards, tea leaf reading, mind reading, and other methods.

- **Spiritism:** Spiritism is a broad word that refers to seeking contact with the spiritual realm. Some primary examples would be those who seek to act as a medium to contact the dead or those who follow a spirit guide. Other examples would be conducting séances, astral projection, channeling, and automatic writing.

- **Sorcery:** Sorcery certainly has similarities to the other categories just mentioned. It has to do with using various means and methods to impact the physical senses with spiritual power. These methods can include spells, magic, various drugs, potions, charms, and incantations.

- **New Age:** The New Age movement is a mixture of various types of religious philosophies and spiritual/occult practices. Some of the activities associated with the New Age movement are eastern/transcendental meditation, reiki healing, spirit guides, crystal healing, hypnotism, and guided imagery.

- **Secret Societies/Cults:** Secret societies are groups that require members to go through initiation rituals and oaths in order to advance to various degrees and stages (this is also true of many satanic and witchcraft groups). A primary example is Freemasonry, a worldwide organization, and its female counterpart, Eastern Star. Examples of cults include Mormonism, Jehovah's Witnesses, Scientology, and Christian Science.

- **Some other activities with occult/new age roots:** yoga, certain martial arts, acupuncture, certain other alternative medical practices.

Deliverance from the Occult

The occult is a powerful force, but it is no match for the name of Jesus. No matter how far into the darkness you are, you can call upon His name and be set free. That being said, breaking free from the occult is not always easy. Jesus has paid the full price for our deliverance, but some may have a hard time cutting occult ties and fully submitting to His lordship. In many cases curses, pacts, and oaths have been made, making it difficult to make a clean break. A person seeking deliverance from the occult must be resolute in their desire to be free and absolutely reliant on the grace of God. Having a loving community of other believers to walk with them through this process is essential.

The following are three keys for making a clean break from the occult and receiving deliverance.

1. Repent

To be delivered, you must repent and let go of any sense of power, control, or influence you think that you gained from the occult. This means that you have a genuine change of heart and mind about the occult and completely turn away from it. You must see it for the sin that it is and truly want to break free of its influence.

The occult is tantamount to idolatry. As the late Bible teacher Derek Prince often put it, it is "looking to satan for that for which we should look to God." To break free from the occult requires genuine repentance. No excuses or justification, even if you got involved "just for fun." No blaming it on others, even if other people drew you in. As part of the repentance process, it may be necessary to forgive people who have hurt you or those who were a part of your journey into the occult. Allow the Holy Spirit to do a deep work inside of you. Don't just hate the symptoms of oppression brought on through your involvement in the occult, hate the very act of sin that the occult is.

2. Renounce

Following repentance is making a full renunciation of anything related to the occult. This means completely severing every tie that you have with it. Acts 19:19 says that "many of those who had practiced magic brought their books together and burned them in the sight of all." This is making a clean break. There is a need to rid yourself of every trace of the occult, including any related materials or objects. It is best to destroy these items, like the example of burning the books of sorcery in this Scripture. Don't keep any items that have occult relationship or ties; the very presence of these items in your house can welcome evil spirits or invite a curse. Deuteronomy 7:26 gives insight into the danger of holding on to accursed items and the attitude that we should have against them: "Nor shall you bring an abomination into your house, lest you be doomed to destruction like it. You shall utterly detest it and utterly abhor it, for it is an accursed thing."

Renouncing the occult will often include leaving behind relationships that tie you to the occult. If there are people with whom you practiced occult activities, it might be necessary to separate yourself from them completely, at least for a time. If you were being taught or mentored in the occult by a leader, you must break your tie with them and renounce any way that you have submitted to them.

Verbalize your renunciation by speaking out a prayer to renounce every occult activity, break every curse, and release yourself from its influence. For example, you can say something like this:

> *In the name of Jesus, I totally renounce my involvement in the occult. I renounce practicing witchcraft, seeing a fortune-teller, reading occult materials (whatever applies specifically to you). I make a clean break and want nothing whatsoever to do with anything that is occult or demonic. Cleanse me in the blood of Jesus from all defilement that has come into my life through occult practices.*

3. Rebuke

Having submitted yourself to God with these steps, you are now in a position to resist the devil. Occult involvement opens the door to evil spirits, and there is a need to cast them out. Rebuke every spirit that is associated with the occult and command them to leave you in the name of Jesus. Keep doing this until there is a sense of complete freedom. There are times when deliverance can be progressive, so be aware that you may need to pray through deliverance on more than one occasion.

In many cases, it is helpful and even necessary to have someone with you to walk through these steps. If you are seeking freedom from the occult, find a trusted friend, pastor, or mentor, and ask them to help you walk through your process of deliverance. Remember: "Whoever calls on the name of the Lord shall be delivered!" (see Joel 2:32 NASB).

| APPENDIX 3 |

A PRAYER FOR DELIVERANCE

As we approach God in prayer for personal deliverance or for ministering to somebody else, it is important that we remember that Jesus has already paid the price for freedom. When He died on the cross and rose from the dead, He defeated the devil and the kingdom of darkness. When we pray for deliverance and take authority over evil spirits, we are simply enforcing what Jesus has already accomplished for us: "He has delivered us from the power of darkness and conveyed us into the kingdom of the Son of His love, in whom we have redemption through His blood, the forgiveness of sins" (Colossians 1:13-14). It is by the blood of Jesus that we come to the Father, and it is by the blood of Jesus that we are forgiven and set free.

I have used prayers like the one in this Appendix on many occasions when ministering deliverance to a person or group of people. If you or someone you know is in need of deliverance, it is an effective tool that can be used to help facilitate the process. The prayer should not be seen as a rigid formula but as a model to follow. The purpose of this prayer is to close all doors, take away any ground that evil spirits may have, and come into complete agreement with God. Once this is done, demons can be cast out.

If you are seeking deliverance for yourself, you can certainly pray through this prayer on your own. But it is also often helpful to have someone, or a small team of two to three people, assist you and pray over you. This is especially true in cases where there is severe demonic influence. Having other people to stand with you in faith and agreement and to command evil spirits to leave can be of tremendous help. If your local church offers deliverance ministry, seek help from a trusted pastor or prayer minister. But again, you can pray through this prayer and receive deliverance by yourself. Indeed, many people have received deliverance this way.

Depending on the nature of your situation, some parts of the prayer may apply and others may not. I always recommend going through the whole prayer and spending more time on the parts that are most applicable. The prayer should be read through slowly, deliberately, and out loud. Take time to allow the Holy Spirit to illuminate anything that needs to be revealed, and customize the prayer as needed. When you come to a blank, fill it in with things that relate to the specifics of your situation.

Once the prayer is finished, continue to welcome the Holy Spirit to minister, and command evil spirits to leave in the name of Jesus until full freedom is found and/or you get to a natural stopping point.

Prayer for Deliverance

1. *Enter into God's presence:*

   Heavenly Father, I come into Your holy presence by the blood of Jesus. Thank You for Your love for me and Your desire to set me free from all demonic influence. I worship and honor You, and I ask that the Holy Spirit would have full control of this time and lead me in prayer. Surround me with Your angels and protect me from all harm.

2. Look to Jesus:

Lord Jesus Christ, I look to You as my only Savior, Healer, and Deliverer. I believe that You are the Son of God and the only way to the Father. I believe that You came in the flesh, died on the cross for my sins, and rose again. I humble myself before You and recognize that it is Your finished work that gives me access to salvation and deliverance.

3. Deal with sin:

Father God, I acknowledge that I have sinned against You and others. I come into the light, confessing my sins before You and holding nothing back. I especially confess _____. I repent of all my sins with a desire to live a life pleasing to You. Purify my heart by the power of the blood of Jesus. Right now I receive Your grace, forgiveness, and cleansing.

4. Forgive others:

I choose to freely forgive anyone who has ever sinned against me or hurt me in any way. I release them to You and let go of all bitterness, anger, hatred, and resentment. Specifically, I forgive _____.

5. Renounce the occult, false teaching, and false religion:

I completely sever myself from all contact that I have ever had with the occult, false religion, and false teaching. I renounce anything to do with witchcraft, divination, sorcery, or New Age philosophy. In particular, I totally renounce _____.

6. **Release from every curse:**

Lord Jesus, thank You for dying on the cross and becoming a curse so that I could be redeemed from every curse and receive God's blessing. Because of Your finished work, I ask You to set me free from every curse that is over my life. I renounce the sins of previous generations and break away from any generational curse that is over my life. Specifically, I break free from the generational curse of _____.
I also break the power of any word curses that have ever been spoken over me. I command any evil spirits associated with word curses to leave me now, in the name of Jesus.

7. **Sever any soul ties:**

I repent of any sexual sin that I have committed and sever any ungodly soul ties that have been created. I set myself free from any unhealthy relationship or ungodly bond to another person. In particular, I break the tie with _____.
I declare that the blood of Jesus separates me from him/her.

8. **Stand with God and against the devil:**

Father God, I align myself with You and want every area of my life to agree with Your Word. I submit myself to You, God, and take an active stand against satan and every one of his demons. By the authority of Jesus' name, I speak to every evil spirit that has any influence in my life and I command you to come out. Go, in the name of Jesus!

As you continue to pray, ask the Lord to give you discernment into what is happening. You may feel clear demonic manifestations happening, and you may sense very obviously when an evil spirit leaves. At the same time, you may not feel anything observable. Keep your eyes on Jesus and trust that the Holy Spirit will lead you. If you are aware of specific evil spirits that have been oppressing you or influencing you, call them out using their specific names. Keep praying until you get to a good stopping point. Then, ask the Holy Spirit to fill you and empower you to walk in freedom.

My Prayer for You

Now I want to pray a prayer over you as you continue your journey in the Lord:

Heavenly Father, I thank You for the person reading this book right now. Thank You for Your love for them and how You paid the price for their salvation and deliverance. I pray Your blessing and protection over them, and that You would guide them into all truth by Your Holy Spirit.

May the power of the Holy Spirit come upon them even now. I take authority over any evil spirits that are influencing their life, and I command them to come out in the name of Jesus! I command every spirit that is from the kingdom of darkness to leave their life right now.

Father, I ask You to fill this person with Your Holy Spirit and empower them to walk in freedom. In Jesus' precious name, amen!

BIBLICAL DECLARATIONS FOR WALKING IN FREEDOM

Why Proclamations?

1. Building your faith: "Faith comes by hearing, and hearing by the word of God" (Romans 10:17). There is power in declaring the Word of God. As you speak the Scriptures and biblical proclamations, expect your faith to grow.

2. Receiving the truth: "You shall know the truth, and the truth shall make you free" (John 8:32). A revelation of truth brings freedom to our lives and delivers us from the lies of the enemy.

3. Renewing your mind: "Do not be conformed to this world, but be transformed by the renewing of your mind" (Romans 12:2). As our minds are renewed by the truth of God's Word, long-term transformation will take place.

4. Fighting the devil: "And take the helmet of salvation, and the sword of the Spirit, which is the word of God" (Ephesians 6:17). The Word of God is a weapon against temptation and against the evil one. Like Jesus did when He was confronted by the devil, we can quote the Word and fight off satan's attacks.

Biblical Proclamations

Make a practice of declaring the following Scriptures and biblical proclamations over your life. Speak them out loud with faith and authority, knowing that you are declaring God's very Word over your life.

> *But God demonstrates His own love toward us, in that while we were still sinners, Christ died for us. Much more then, having now been justified by His blood, we shall be saved from wrath through Him. For if when we were enemies we were reconciled to God through the death of His Son, much more, having been reconciled, we shall be saved by His life* (Romans 5:8-10).

Proclamation: I am absolutely loved by God and have been reconciled to Him through Christ's death. Jesus died in my place; and because His blood covers me, God looks at me and declares me righteous. I am free from all guilt, shame, wrath, and condemnation.

> *He has delivered us from the power of darkness and conveyed us into the kingdom of the Son of His love, in whom we have redemption through His blood, the forgiveness of sins* (Colossians 1:13-14).

Proclamation: I have been delivered from the kingdom of darkness and now belong to the Kingdom of God. I am redeemed by the blood of Jesus, and satan has no hold on my life. Because the blood of Jesus was shed for me, I am completely forgiven of all of my sins.

Behold, I give you the authority to trample on serpents and scorpions, and over all the power of the enemy, and nothing shall by any means hurt you. Nevertheless do not rejoice in this, that the spirits are subject to you, but rather rejoice because your names are written in heaven (Luke 10:19-20).

Proclamation: In Christ I have been given authority over every evil spirit, and no demon will harm me. I trample on all of the works of the devil because of the finished work of Jesus. Demons are subject to me in the name of Jesus. I rejoice that my name is written in Heaven, that my life belongs to God, and that I am His child.

Christ has redeemed us from the curse of the law, having become a curse for us (for it is written, "Cursed is everyone who hangs on a tree"), that the blessing of Abraham might come upon the Gentiles in Christ Jesus, that we might receive the promise of the Spirit through faith (Galatians 3:13-14).

Proclamation: Because Jesus became a curse for me on the cross, I am set free from every curse. I will not live under the power of any curse because I have been redeemed by Christ. I am blessed and will walk in all of the blessings that God has for me. I receive the Holy Spirit into my life and will walk in His power and love.

And the God of peace will crush Satan under your feet shortly... (Romans 16:20).

...For this purpose the Son of God was manifested, that He might destroy the works of the devil (1 John 3:8).

Proclamation: The God of peace crushes satan under my feet. Jesus came to destroy the works of the devil, and I declare that every work of the evil one is destroyed in my life. Satan is totally defeated, and I am completely victorious in Christ.

Therefore submit to God. Resist the devil and he will flee from you (James 4:7).

Proclamation: I submit myself completely to God and declare that Jesus is Lord of my entire life. I take an active stand against the devil, and he flees from me.

God has not given us a spirit of fear, but of power and of love and of a sound mind (2 Timothy 1:7).

Proclamation: I am not subject to the spirit of fear, anxiety, or intimidation. God's perfect love casts out all fear, and He has filled me with the love and power of the Holy Spirit. My mind is clear, sound, and at peace.

Be anxious for nothing, but in everything by prayer and supplication, with thanksgiving, let your requests be made known to God; and the peace of God, which surpasses all understanding, will guard your hearts and minds through Christ Jesus (Philippians 4:6-7).

Proclamation: I will not be anxious or worried about anything, but will cast my cares upon the Lord in prayer. Instead of being anxious, I will give thanks to God and trust in Him. God's peace protects my heart and mind, even when I don't understand my circumstances.

I will both lie down in peace, and sleep; for You alone, O Lord, make me dwell in safety (Psalm 4:8).

Proclamation: I declare that my sleep belongs to the Lord, and that He gives me rest. I will have peace in the night and will sleep without fear or torment.

Inasmuch then as the children have partaken of flesh and blood, He Himself likewise shared in the same, that through death He might destroy him who had the power of death, that is, the devil, and release those who through fear of death were all their lifetime subject to bondage (Hebrews 2:14-15).

Proclamation: By His death on the cross, Jesus has destroyed the devil and has defeated death. I will not be subject to the fear of death any longer, for my life is in God's hands. I have been given abundant life in Christ and will walk in this life.

Therefore, if anyone is in Christ, he is a new creation; old things have passed away; behold, all things have become new (2 Corinthians 5:17).

Proclamation: I am a new creation in Christ, identified with His death, burial, resurrection, and ascension. I will not be defined by or bound by my past, and I will not be held back in my destiny.

ABOUT JAKE KAIL

Jake Kail was called to ministry in college after a life-changing encounter with God. He is passionate for the presence of God and to see His Kingdom come and will be done "on earth as it is in heaven."

Jake is the author of multiple books, including *Setting Captives Free* and *Hypocrisy Exposed*. He speaks at churches, conferences, retreats, and other events, preaching and teaching with a demonstration of the Holy Spirit's power.

Jake lives in Lancaster, Pennsylvania, with his wife, Anna, and their kids, and serves as the lead pastor of Threshold Church.

Visit Jake's ministry website and blog:

www.jakekail.com

Follow Jake on Twitter:

@JakeKail

Like Jake's page on Facebook:

www.facebook.com/JakeKailAuthor

Follow Jake on Instagram:

@jake_kail